16 AMAZING STORIES
of Divine Intervention

Includes stories about two U.S. Presidents,
a Hollywood Icon, famous athletes, rock musicians,
a former gang leader, a former witch
and other remarkable lives

JAMES L. ("LEE") LAMBERT

Acknowledgments and Dedication

I want to extend my sincere thanks to my wife, Lorraine Lambert, who has been such an important part of this project. Lori has spent countless hours reviewing and editing chapters of this book. She has dedicated her time and energy in help making this work the best it can be. Lori's loving support is greatly appreciated and acknowledged. I would like to thank Dr. Larry Keefauver for his valuable assistance as well.

Sixteen Amazing Stories is dedicated to my mother, C. Joanne Lambert who passed away into the arms of her loving Savior in February of 2006. While I miss her greatly, I know she is especially happy to be again with my dad, James L. Lambert III. I will never forget finding a marker in her backyard after my dad's death that read, "If tears could build a stairway and memories a lane, I'd walk right up to Heaven and bring you home again." If anything crystallized my mom's feelings towards my dad this simple marker said it all.

My mom was a sweet person and later in her life finally said, "Yes," to her loving Savior, Jesus Christ. She was an inspiration to me. She taught me the importance of being kind and appreciative of life. My mom went out of her way to encourage me when I needed support. About six months after her passing, I found an old letter which my mother never got around to sending me when I was in college, years before. The letter still had an unused a six-cent stamp on it. In it, the correspondence was filled with endearing words of encouragement that I needed, especially at that time. I will never forget the moment when I found this special gift from God. It was a blessing from Heaven.

My mom is missed by her family to this day and this book is dedicated to her. I hope that I can pass on the spirit of encouragement to the readers of this book and touch their lives just as I was touched by my mother.

Table of Contents

Preface
16 Amazing Stories of Divine Intervention

Isn't God amazing? To me, it's simply mind boggling to see just how far God will go for anyone who shows even the slightest inclination of wanting to have a personal relationship with the Creator of the Universe. All four Gospels (the book of Matthew, Mark, Luke and John from the Bible) show us that the Heavenly Father will lovingly pursue anyone who desires to know Him. God wants to have that closeness with each one of us, but only if we are willing. Being a perfect gentleman, He will not force Himself on us regardless of who we are, where we are, or what we are doing.

Certainly this was true for me. In my formative years I participated in Sunday school at the local Presbyterian Church due to the nudging of my dad. I missed the gospel message and quickly lost interest. However, my neighbor, Max Foresman, (a retired executive and former Army chaplain during World War II), prayed and planted a seed of faith in me during those years. Max regularly imparted his sage advice and sometimes even talked about God. I also suspect my Grandmother, Charlotte Von Steuben Lees, (fondly called Ama by her grandchildren), was likely praying for me as well.

My high school years were a happy time. My parents had given me a solid foundation of social skills, but they lacked spiritual insight. By the time I entered the second semester of my freshman year in college, I made the mistake of associating with the wrong crowd and made some poor choices. I began to use drugs and became a lost person in my own lost world.

While on a surfing holiday to Santa Cruz, CA, I was involved in a terrible car accident. I look back on that November day and am still in disbelief that I didn't lose my right leg when my '69 Ford van collided head-on into a guard rail. The rail rammed through my van like a spear. That became a defining moment for me, and for the next three or four months I began questioning my own mortality and the direction my life was taking.

Little did I know that I had friends (Charmaine and Larry Allen) from my small college in Oregon who were praying for me. Through a chain of events that I would not totally comprehend until years later, my life was about to change. On one incredible Friday night Larry came to my dormitory room and for about 15 minutes read some simple Biblical truths and quotes that were condensed in a Campus Crusade for Christ booklet entitled, the Four Spiritual Laws. For the first time in my life, the Biblical message of salvation was clearly presented to me. Deep down in my heart, I knew that Christ was who He said He was. I knew by His death on the cross, my sins would be covered with His grace.

On that February night, I came to the end of myself and turned to the one person who would forever change my life: Jesus Christ. I distinctly remember running several blocks from my dormitory that night after I had made my decision for Christ and looked into the dark, star studded sky, knowing beyond a shadow of a doubt that a wonderful peace and presence had just entered my life.

In our conversation that night, Larry encouraged me to read the Bible (starting with the Gospel of John). I also realized that I needed to find a church to attend – but which church, I had no idea. My girl-friend (and future wife, Lori) and I finally visited the nearest church we knew of. When the church service began, we heard a young girl (whose name was Chris Friesen) sing a song about the blood of Christ. I thought to myself, what kind of a church would sing about blood of all things. I thought it was weird but something told me to be polite to the family whose daughter had just sung the song. At the end of the service, the young girl's parents (Frank and Adina Friesen) introduced themselves to us.

A little more than two weeks later, I happened to see Chris's mother in a local store. She immediately sought me out and invited me to her home. I accepted. Little did I know that my new friendship with the Friesen family would also have a profound and a positive influence on my young life.

The Friesens were devout Christians from the province of Manitoba, Canada. Coming from a strict Mennonite background, the couple was spiritually renewed by the charismatic movement during those days. Their renewed zeal and faith in Christ had encouraged the family to leave their Canadian hometown and immigrate to the United States. In their move south through northwestern Oregon, Chris' mother felt that God was urging them to settle down in the small town of McMinnville. The town, located one hour's drive from the Oregon coast, was home to Linfield College, a small Pacific Northwest school founded in 1859, which "happened" to be the school I was attending.

My new friends not only invited me and Lori to come over to their home but they welcomed many dozens of college students for several years into their home for bible study. The Friesen's home was a second home to many students from the college who were away from their family for the first time. In all the many prayer meetings and Bible studies for college kids that spring and fall, I can think of at least four people (Stephen Schrater, Nick Burt, Tim McGill, and Bob Prouty) who eventually went into full time Christian service. Do I believe it was just a 'coincidence' this couple left their home in Canada to move across the street from the college campus? No. Do I think God is real? Yes! He has made Himself real to me and He will continue to reach out to anyone who seeks Him today.

The stories in this book will demonstrate just how real God is to anyone who opens their heart and honestly seeks Him.

What you are about to read are true stories about people who have some extraordinary talents, and yet as humans they have strengths and weaknesses; successes and failures. They make some wise decisions and some that are not so wise. What they all share in common, however, is that they all experienced a moment of surrender to the God of the universe.

Chapter 1

Mickey Mantle: His Ninth-Inning Miracle

W hat made Mickey Mantle a sports icon? Was it his talent, strength, charisma, determination, passion for baseball, teamwork, sense of adventure, persistence or could there be more? All of these attributes brought crowds to their feet in wild applause when he walked onto the field. He celebrated much success; but he also groveled in the lows of his losses. Perhaps in working through our shortcomings, we learn to better appreciate our successes.

Mickey Mantle, the oldest of four siblings entered this world with a hearty cry on October 20, 1931 and spent the first few years of his toddler days in Spavinal, Oklahoma. His father, Elvin 'Mutt' Mantle, named him after the famous Philadelphia Athletics and Detroit Tigers' catcher, Mickey Cochrane. After a few years, Elvin and Lovell Mantle moved to a modest home in Commerce, Oklahoma that had neither electricity nor running water.

As a zinc miner, Mickey's father had a hard life. Yet even after days spent deep in the mines, Mutt routinely played with his son and taught him the intricacies of baseball. Mickey's dad loved the sport. It wasn't unusual for Mutt to spend hours pitching, catching and throwing balls with Mickey. Mutt even whittled down his own broken wood bats so that his son could use them in practice.

Mutt was consumed with baseball, and during the weekends he loved playing semi-pro baseball. He adored the sport yet adored his son even more. Mutt had his own personal dreams of playing baseball someday as a major leaguer, yet worked tirelessly to improve Mickey's baseball skills. As Mickey told Sports Illustrated magazine in 1994, "I loved my father, although I couldn't tell him that, just like he couldn't tell me. He put his arm around me and hugged me, but he'd be playing a joke at the same time, kicking me in the butt with his foot. But I knew he loved me." [1]

At a fairly early age, Mickey was touched by death in his own family. In his book, All My Octobers, Mantle said, "By the time I was 13, my grandpa Charlie and my two uncles ... had died of Hodgkin's"disease. [2] It was a hard pill to swallow and left a deep impression on the young boy. Those events, however, did not slow him down, for by the time he was fifteen Mickey was regularly playing baseball with players older than himself.

In high school Mickey was quite the athlete and played baseball, basketball and football. He was even offered a football scholarship to the University of Oklahoma. While in his junior year, the shy teenager from Commerce, Oklahoma, was spotted by professional baseball scout, Tom Greenwade. This was to change his life forever. [3]

Agape Press reported, "Greenwade went to a game in Kansas with the intention of scouting another player from Mantle's team. Instead, the sixteen-year-old Mantle, an outfielder on the Baxter-Springs team, drew the attention of the veteran Yankee scout. The young Mantle dazzled Greenwade and the spectators that day. Incredibly, Mickey hit two very long home runs while playing against baseball players several years older than the aspiring switch-hitter from Commerce, Oklahoma." The same report went on to say that "Greenwade was surprised when he found out Mantle's age. He knew he couldn't offer the talented teen a professional contract until he had finished high school. Still, he promised he would return when Mantle graduated." The veteran scout noted that he "knew the player he had found was as talented as any young prospect he had ever seen." [4]

Every sports story has some kind of love story in the mix and Mickey's was no different. On October 6, 1949, a cheerleader, Meryln Johnson, saw Mickey for the first time at a high school football game. Within a few days, the young baseball player asked her out for a date.

It didn't take long for Meryln to develop strong feelings for Mickey. She expounded later in her book, A Hero All His Life, "I developed an instant crush on Mickey Mantle, and by our second or third date, I was in love with him and always would be." [5]

True to his word the Yankees' scout Greenwade returned to Oklahoma upon Mantle's graduation and signed him to a professional contract. It was an exciting day in the Mantle household. For the next few seasons Mickey played in the minor leagues, but by 1951 he was called up to the American league to play for the New York Yankees.

When the young slugger was promoted to the team, the Yankees had already appeared in seventeen World Series with thirteen wins. A number of famous baseball stars had played for the well known franchise (including Babe Ruth, Lou Gehrig, Bill Dickey, Toni Lazzeri, and Joe DiMaggio to name a few). On April 17, 1951, Mickey played his first major league game. On that day he played right field, next to the legendary Yankee center fielder, Joe DiMaggio and went one for four.

The pressures and expectations on this young player were rough. When Mickey experienced a batting slump during his first major league season, he was dispatched back to their minor leagues. Sports Illustrated said, "He was so depressed he talked about quitting the game. That's when his father famously drove up to Kansas City and started packing his clothes and, as Mickey recalled said, "I thought I raised a man. I see I raised a coward instead. You can come back to Oklahoma and work the mines with me." [6] Those comments had a lasting effect on the nineteen-year old. Mickey dearly loved his father. Now, he would prove to everyone including his father that he belonged in the majors. Mickey stayed, and after just forty games in the minors, Mantle was back in a Yankee uniform.

The Yankees were making their eighteenth trip to the World Series against the National League champion in October of 1951. The Giants, representing the National League, had won their pennant in a dramatic fashion. It was the first World Series for two up and coming stars: the Giants Willie Mays and Mantle. It was during his first World Series that Mantle's career almost ended. To avoid colliding with DiMaggio in the outfield, Mantle shifted and caught his shoe spike on the tip of a sprinkler. It sounds so simple yet it resulted in emergency knee surgery for the young outfielder.

Mickey noticed his father's frail physical condition when he came to visit his son. Mickey learned from his father's doctor that Mutt had Hodgkin's disease. First, his grandfather Charlie and two uncles, now it was attacking his father—his closest friend. While the news of Mutt's illness was a severe blow to the young outfielder, his upcoming marriage to Merlyn Johnson became a source of comfort. It helped that Mutt approved. Why wouldn't he? Merlyn's family were church going folks and she had been brought up in a religious home.[7] Her father and grandfather were deacons in the Baptist church.[8] The couple married December 23, 1951.[9]

Making the switch from living in Oklahoma to New York City was a challenging experience for the newlyweds. On May 6, 1952, team manager, Casey Stengel, broke the news of Mutt's death to Mickey. Mickey confessed to Sports Illustrated years later that when his father died, "I was devastated and that's when I started drinking. I guess alcohol helped me escape the pain of losing him."[10] He went on to say, "When my father died, Casey became like a father to me."[11]

But the game must go on! The beginning of the 1952 season brought with it high expectations for the New York team. Just last October the Yankees had come off another World Series victory. The fans could feel the electricity in the air. All was good—or was it?

Life on the road became difficult for Mickey's young wife, Merlyn. Travel for a major league baseball player in the 1950s was much different than it is today with its corporate jets and limousines. An away schedule often kept the family separated for weeks at a time. Loneliness, alcohol and acts of indiscretion ruined many marriages. Temptation was everywhere and what time they had away from practice was spent socializing.

Mickey felt a lot of pressure because his team was expected to repeat their previous year's championship performance. Mantle later confessed that he made the mistake of not properly rehabilitating his knee from his 1951 World Series injury. Regardless, in '52, the young outfielder had a stellar season batting .311 with twenty-three home runs.

After winning another American League title in the fall of 1952, the Yankees turned their attention to defending their World Championship title against their cross-town rival and National League champs, Brooklyn Dodgers. By the seventh game, the series was tied, 3-3. The major league (MLB) world championship game came down to nine innings of play. The Dodgers were a powerful team made up of stars like Jackie Robinson, Duke Snider, Roy Campanella, Pee Wee Reese and Gil Hodges. By the sixth inning of that deciding seventh game, the score was tied.

Every run, every hit and every catch mattered. Joe Black was the opposing Brooklyn pitcher. After one out, Mantle came to the plate. Black pitched him a slider and wham! Mickey nailed the ball. The ball was hit so hard that it went over the right field scoreboard and won the game for them. In his book, All My Octobers, Mantle explained how he was personally touched by Jackie Robinson's comments to the media after the game. Jackie flatly said that "Mantle beat us. He was the difference between the two teams. They didn't miss (Joe) DiMaggio."11 It also didn't hurt that Yankees second baseman Billy Martin made a spectacular game-saving catch as well. After their dramatic win at Ebbets field, it became clear to everyone that the Yankees had found the replacement for their retired star, Joe DiMaggio.

By the end of the season, Mickey and Merlyn left their small apartment in NYC and traveled back to Oklahoma. Receiving a World Series check was becoming a nice habit for the Yankee outfielder. That fall Merlyn was thrilled when her husband was honored by his home town of Commerce, Oklahoma with a parade.

As for the '53 season, Mickey's team was determined to keep their record alive by winning the fifth straight American league pennant. It was during an early April exhibition game in Brooklyn that Mantle discovered, thanks to a public address announcer, that he was the new father of a baby boy, Mickey Jr. It was also during the first week of the season that Mantle hit one of his most memorable home runs. Mantle was at the plate when Chuck Stobbs of the Washington Senators threw a chest-high fastball. Mantle got all of it. He crushed the ball so hard it careened off a beer sign located on the scoreboard behind sixty-five feet of outfield bleachers. A young boy found the ball in the yard of a home on Oakdale Street. The sign the ball hit was sixty feet high and was located at the rear of the stadium. Just to clear the outfield fence Mantle's hit had to first travel 391 feet. Considering the trajectory of the ball, a witness calculated it traveled 565 feet.

In September, during the '53 season, in a game against the Detroit Tigers, Mickey hit yet another towering home run. The famous HR hit the upper deck of the stadium. Again, based on the trajectory of the ball, a baseball expert calculated the ball would have traveled 620 feet, had it not hit the inside of the upper deck. The season culminated with the Yankees winning the American league pennant.

That fall, and for the second time in center-fielder's young career, his team would again face the National League champions, the Dodgers. The first and second games were won by the American league champions, 9-5 and 4-2, respectively. Game three, played at Ebbets field in Brooklyn, was a completely different story. Dodger pitcher, Carl Erskine struck out fourteen Yankees in a sterling performance. His team went on to win the third game 3-2. By game four, the Dodgers posted another win, tying the series. The fans were wild with anticipation!

Game five was the pivotal game of the 1953 Series. With Mickey's team holding onto a slim lead, the center-fielder arrived at the plate in the third inning facing Dodger pitcher Russ Meyer. Batting from his left side, Mickey firmly stroked the reliever's first pitch, sending it high over the left field fence. What a display of talent and strength! With his home-run in the fifth game, Mickey would join only three other players in World Series history to hit a grand slam. The Yanks went on to win the series in the sixth to win another World Championship for the popular New York baseball club. [12]

Billy Martin, a fellow teammate, and Mickey had at this point become good friends. The fiery second baseman and Mickey were also away game roommates, and both enjoyed their alcohol. Mickey's wife was not happy about this habit and years later it eventually affected other family members as well. Mickey admitted in an interview with Sports Illustrated that if his father hadn't died so young, he would have been there to discourage his son from using alcohol.

During the 1954 season, Mickey's team experienced something that hadn't happened since he first put on the pinstripes. His team didn't win an American league pennant. The New York team placed second behind a Cleveland Indian team that had a remarkable pitching staff. The setback was incentive enough for the team to buckle down and get back to basics instead of riding on the coattails of their five-year winning streak (1949-1953).

The following year in 1955, the Yankees won another American league pennant. Their cross town rivals, the Dodgers, were again opponents from the rival league. That year, the Brooklyn team was a formidable opponent for the Bronx bombers. Their new manager, Walter Alston, had a dangerous club that featured star players like (P) Don Newsome, (C) Roy Campanella, (OF) Duke Snider, (OF) Junior Gilliam, (1B) Gil Hodges, (SS) Pee Wee Reese and (2B) Jackie Robinson. Mantle suffered an injury that significantly hurt his team. The Dodgers won the series in game seven with a dramatic catch by right fielder, Sandy Amoros. It was a dream come true for the Brooklyn fans. The Brooklyn team had finally won their first championship since the World Series began in 1903. [13]

Licking his wounds, Mantle used his off-season time reassessing his life, skills, and future with the New York team.

That winter Merlyn presented her husband Mickey with a special present- their second son, David who was born on December 26, 1955. Now with two young sons, he was even more torn with all the pressures and long absences required for training. Yet, when spring training finally rolled around again, Mickey was physically prepared for another memorable season. He got it in 1956!

Mickey's '56 campaign was one of the greatest individual seasons any player would ever experience. Since 1901 there had only been nine triple crown winners in the American League. (There were even fewer, (six), in the National League). Winning the triple crown meant having the highest individual batting average, highest number of RBIs (runs batted in) and HRs (home runs) – all in the same season. In 1956, Mantle had fifty-two home runs, 130 RBIs to go along with a .353 batting average. With this accomplishment, the young center-fielder was standing next to the likes of Nap Lajoie, Ty Cobb,

Jimmy Foxx, Lou Gerhig and Ted Williams in the record books. Just to show how difficult it is to obtain this feat, the last time the triple crown was won in the American League was in 1967, and the last time it was done in the National League was 1937.

Mantle was also voted the league's most valuable player that year. His team broke the club season HR record by smashing 190 home runs. The Yankees won the pennant and the series again featured the rivalry up between the Yanks and the Brooklyn Dodgers.[14] The series is perhaps best known for the fifth game, played on October 8, 1956. That was the day that Yankee pitcher, Don Larsen, pitched a perfect game (holding Brooklyn to no hits, no walks and no runs scored). It was a feat that had never happened in the championship game before and may never occur again. Two great teams battled it out that October with Mickey's Yankees winning four games to three.[15]

The Yankees continued their fabulous run, representing the American League again with appearances in the next two (1957 and 1958) October championship games. In 1957, the Milwaukee Braves were led by the baseball legends Henry 'Hank' Aaron, Eddie Mathews, Warren Spahn and Lew Burdette. That year also showed some roster changes for the Yankees. Mickey's long time friend, Billy Martin was traded to make way for new talent. It was rumored that Yankee management somehow felt that the colorful second baseman was a bad influence on Mantle. A young, talented infielder by the name of Bobby Richardson would play extensively during that '57 season. The team also acquired a catcher by the name of Elston Howard and a first baseman named Tony Kubeck. Clearly, the Yankee organization was going through some personnel and personal changes. However, despite the loss of his good friend, leg problems and occasional injuries, Mickey hit .365 during the regular season.

By the end of the '58 season, the Yankees again found themselves in another championship series with the Braves. Despite playing in the hostile environment of Milwaukee Stadium in game six, Mickey's team rallied for a dramatic 4-3 victory in the tenth inning. In the deciding seventh game with a 6-2 victory, Casey Stengel, nicknamed "the old professor" and his team, were once again back on top of the baseball world.[16] From 1949 to 1958, the Yankees appeared in nine World Series, missing the fall classic only once in 1954.

By November, Mickey had something else for which to be thankful. His wife Merlyn gave birth to their third son, Billy, born on Thanksgiving Day, 1958.

During the late 1950s, Mickey, and his old friend (pitcher) Whitey Ford, were the leaders of the Bronx club. Nevertheless, that number seven jersey seemed to be a magnet for injuries. Even during his best years as the Yankee center-fielder, Mickey found it hard to cope with some of the physical aliments he had acquired. He later admitted in a Sports Illustrated article that he would cover the pain and drown his concerns by drinking alcohol. Mantle justified his behavior with the saying, "If you were going to be The Man on the field, you had to be The Man off the field." [17]

The Yankees' four-year run as American League champions ended in 1959. It was a disappointing season for the Yankee's star player. He continued to battle ankle and shoulder injuries and hit under .300 for the first time since 1953. The White Sox had won their first pennant in four decades, ultimately losing to the Los Angeles Dodgers in the World Series. Much to the chagrin of the loyal Brooklyn fans, Dodger owner Walter O'Malley moved their beloved team to Los Angeles.

During that year Mickey's Yankees picked up a quality third baseman by the name of Clete Boyer. As the 1960 season approached, management traded for outfielder Roger Maris, and by the end of the 1960 season, they were atop the American League standings. In Detroit, Mickey hit another 'tape measure' home run that cleared the roof of Tiger's stadium (with an estimated distance of more than 660 feet).

In March of that year, Merlyn bore a fourth son, Danny. Most of us cannot even imagine what the personal life of a professional player might entail. We only see him in his uniform and blasting the ball out of the stadium to break old records. From an editorial review of the Mantles' book, A Hero All His Life, it was reported, "The ballplayer was almost always on the road, either playing baseball or starring on the lecture circuit. He became an open womanizer, in two instances engaging in long-term affairs about which his wife knew.

As the Mantle sons grew up, they became their father's drinking partners. All of them developed alcohol and/or drug addictions and were treated at the Betty Ford Clinic. Mickey is quoted as saying he was a poor husband and father, an assessment readers will consider accurate, but his family expresses only love for him and recalls the qualities that endeared him to them" Publisher's Weekly (1996). It is very obvious that he had many struggles but it is even more obvious that he tried to overcome them both on the field and at home.

After the birth of Danny, Mantle returned to training with a different attitude. As the father of four handsome sons, he was ready to take on the world! The 1960 Pirates, who had not won a series since 1927, were a scrappy NL winning team and featured players such as Dick Groat, Roberto Clemente, Bill Virdon, Vernon Law, Dick Stuart and Bill Mazeroski. Mantle believed that the Pirate's second baseman's swing of the bat on October 13, 1960, likely was the reason Casey Stengel's contract wasn't renewed that year.

Few can remember a series where there was such a disparaging difference of runs scored from the losing team (i.e. 55 runs scored by the loosing Yankees vs. 27 runs scored by the winning Pirates and 60 total hits by the winning Pirates vs. 91 hits by the Yankees.) The mere fact that the Yankees second baseman, Bobby Richardson was the only winning Series MVP from the losing team should speak volumes. Even with pitching, the Yankees team ERA was significantly better (3.54 team ERA vs. team winning ERA 7.11 for the Pirates). It's no wonder that Mantle later would say that the outcome of the 1960 Series was, professionally, "the worst disappointment of (his) baseball career." [18]

Certainly Mickey's "Bronx Bombers" had a lot of incentive going for them for the upcoming season and 1961 would go down as one of the most exciting baseball seasons in history. Mickey and close friend, Roger Maris, held their fans and the media captive by staging a season-long duel to see who would break Babe Ruth's record of sixty home runs. The record had stood the test of time for thirty four years. Combined, the two Yankee stars (the "M and M boys") would hit a team record 115 home runs. On the last day of the regular season Roger Maris would make headlines by hitting his 61st HR in the fourth inning. Yankee catcher, Yogi Berra, would later say in Our Mickey, cherished memories of an American Icon, "If Mantle "hadn't (gotten hurt), they both would have passed the Babe, I think.'" [19]

The World Series with the Cincinnati Reds was almost anti-climatic. The unexpected heroes of the series showed just how deep the NY roster really was. Mantle's injuries forced him to have only six "at bats." Maris was not his usual self, collecting only two hits in nineteen times at bat. Bill Showron, Bobby Richardson, Johnny Blanchard and Hector Lopez carried much of the load for the team that would bring another World Championship (4-1) to New York. [20]

Mantle experienced a good season in 1962. He not only collected another American league MVP title, he was on his way to his tenth World Series. Even though the National league Champions had moved to San Francisco, Mickey enjoyed the challenge of playing his old cross-town rivals. In the final game with two out and the game on the line, Yankee second baseman Bobby Richardson made a leaping catch and snuffed out the Giants chance for a dramatic comeback. The celebration was on.

However, the injuries continued to take their toll on the thirty-one year old center-fielder. Since 1960, the "M & M boys" were the toast of Manhattan. Mantle and Maris had shined during their regular seasons but their luck usually turned tail and went south when October rolled around. That pattern didn't change in 1963. Mickey's friend was benched for the rest of the series when he ran into a railing after chasing down a ball in the outfield.

Mishaps were a problem for the Yankee center-fielder along with many of his teammates during the 1963 season. In early June, Mickey had a foot and knee injury that caused him to miss sixty one games. In his first appearance back from the injury, Mantle hit a home run that tied a game against the Orioles with the home team going on to win 11-10. In his book, All My Octobers, Mickey described the exhilarating experience before his cheering, applauding, home-town fans. Can't you hear the roar? Mantle ended the season with only 172 at bats, but hit over .300 for the ninth time in his career with his team again winning the American League pennant.

The National League champion Los Angeles Dodgers, were a much different team than their predecessors from Brooklyn. Many of the old stars were gone only to be replaced by new ones including record breaking, base-stealer Maury Wills, batting champion Tommy Davis, Frank Howard, Johnny Roseboro, reliever Ron Perranoski, pitchers Sandy Koufax and Don Drysdale. Johnny Podres, a star from Brooklyn's 1955 championship team, was still in Dodger blue. That year, NY traded Mickey's friend and former teammate, Bill Skowron, to Los Angeles. The Dodgers had an intimidating pitching staff that worked its magic on the Yanks. In 1963, the NY team had a poultry World Series .171 batting average. In the fourth game, NY made a last ditch effort to gain respect when Mantle hit a homer off Koufax in the seventh inning. Los Angeles recovered the lead when Joe Pepitone committed a third base error and Junior Gilliam scored on a deeply hit ball to Mantle. The Dodgers 4-0 sweep of the series was a disappointing ending to the Yankees season and especially to Mantle.[21]

When important games are lost, personnel changes always occur and Yogi Berra replaced Ralph Houk as the team manager in 1964. At first some of the players questioned some of Berra's on the field moves but New York ended up making a strong push that September, winning eleven straight games to win the 1964 American league pennant by one game. Mickey again had a stellar year, batting over .300 for the tenth time. As one of the most popular players in major league baseball, Mantle, at the age of thirty two, was now commanding a salary of $100,000 a year. That was a lot of money in 1964 but nothing compared to salaries today.

The National League champions, St. Louis Cardinals made their first World Series appearance after a dry spell of eighteen years in 1964. The Cardinal stars of yesteryear (Stan Musial, Enos Slaughter, Red Schoendienst and Joe Garagiola) were gone and replaced by a new, talented group of players (Lou Brock, Curt Flood, Bob Gibson and Tim McCarver). Game one was a disappointment for the Yankees when their starting pitcher, Whitey Ford, had arm problems. After losing game one, Berra turned rookie Mel Stottlemyre loose to the pitching mound. The Yankee pitcher did well in beating a very good opponent, Bob Gibson. In game three, Mantle lit the scoreboard with a dramatic home run in the ninth inning to the cheers of over 65,000 New York fans. The Cardinals won the next two games (4-3 and 5-2) showing how closely matched the two teams really were. The World Championship again came down to the seventh and deciding game. By the end of the fifth inning the Cardinals jumped off to a 6-0 lead. [22] A late inning New York rally wasn't enough to overcome St. Louis' early lead. That final game was a sad time for the aging all-star outfielder.

By the end of the 1964 season, the Yankees had appeared in twelve World Series since the time Mickey first joined the club in 1951. During that remarkable stretch, they won seven World Championships. Clearly, it was a feat that many believe will never be equaled in all of sports. Mickey Mantle had also established himself as the all-time World Series home run king.

An era had ended. By 1965, Mantle's batting average had fallen to .255. The years of injuries to his cartilage and weakened bones in his legs had taken their toll. Years later Mickey would admit that his long term struggles with alcohol prevented him from properly rehabbing his body and attending to his baseball-related injuries. This would cause baseball enthusiasts to ponder; just how much farther could Mantle have gone if he had been free of injuries? One can only speculate.

The Yankees had lost much of the magic the team had in the '50s and early '60s. For the next three years (between 1965 and 1967) the Yankees had losing seasons. Agape Press shared, "During their years with the Yankees, the seven time all-star second baseman (Bobby Richardson) had many opportunities to share his faith with Mantle. It appeared at the time that Mickey never really took Richardson's words of spiritual encouragement to heart." [23]

Years later, Richardson disclosed to the Christian Broadcasting Network that he "remembered a dozen times when he and I spent time together (with Mickey) ... and talked about the things in life that really mattered, his relationship with Christ." A series of providential coincidences years later answered the prayers of Mantle's team-mate and friend.

Despite Mantle's injuries during those years, he was elected to the American all-star team two more times (in 1967 and 1968).

By 1967, Mickey moved to first base when his coach, Ralph Houk, assigned Joe Pepitone to play centerfield. Houk was convinced that the change would help the aging star and benefit the team. With these changes, the New York club began to see their fortunes reverse in 1968. Mantle hit his 535th home run of the season on a lob pitch by Denny McClain. McClain and his pennant-winning team had so much respect for their legendary opponent that he wanted to send him out right. [24] On September 20, 1968, Mickey hit his last home run (#536) against the Boston Red Sox pitcher, Jim Lonborg.

Mickey announced his retirement from professional baseball on March 1, 1969. That day, baseball lost a great player. Yankee fans would come to appreciate many of the accomplishments of their aging star. Mantle's baseball stats (slugging percentage, on base average, runs scored, RBI's and home runs) were impressive. It's no wonder that 'the Mick' was an all-star sixteen times during the eighteen years he was in baseball.

On June 8, 1969 the Yankee organization retired his #7 jersey. It was a time of reflection for the retired baseball great. He would no longer come to the stadium for team meetings, regular work-outs or games. His professional baseball playing days were over. Mantle openly shared, "After the '68 season I went home to Dallas and began to think about what I would do with the rest of my life." [25]

By 1970, Mantle was offered a first base coaching job with his former team. His stint as a coach would only last one season. In his first year of eligibility (in 1984) Mickey was nominated into the Baseball Hall of Fame. It was a great honor for the player from Commerce, OK.

Mickey also kept in touch with his former teammate and friend, Bobby Richardson. The former Yankee second baseman said, "On numerous occasions Mickey would help me with various (outside) interests I was involved in." [26] "Mantle participated 'in sports banquets, fund raisers for the YMCA and even a baseball instructional film event' from the University of South Carolina, where Richardson was head coach in the 1970s." [27]

Mantle also became involved in business ventures that included a personnel agency with Jets' quarterback, Joe Namath. He also lent his name to a food establishment, however it wasn't until 1988 when

Mickey Mantle's Restaurant and Sports Bar in NYC actually opened. (By all indications, the New York eatery in the city was still thriving as of 2011)

Continued partying and drinking that first started in the 50's were wreaking havoc with the retired star's health. Mickey realized that his growing dependency on alcohol was troubling not only to his family but to friends around him. He freely admitted in a Sports Illustrated cover story, "Drinking (had) become an all too frequent routine for me," saying that he "used alcohol as a crutch." [28]

Mickey's wife, Merlyn, was also having a difficult time enduring the ups and downs of a turbulent relationship. Not only was alcohol a problem for Mickey but it had become a serious issue for her as well. She started drinking to ease her pain when she "discovered the first of what I learned was a string of Mick's affairs." [29]

Mantle took on a job representing the Claridge Hotel in Atlantic City in 1983. His association with the gambling casino was condemned by baseball commissioner, Bowie Kuhn. Mickey's family was experiencing some turbulent times. His son, Billy, was suffering from Hodgkins Disease that was first diagnosed in 1977. What complicated his son's condition was an addiction to pain pills. To add more stress, Mickey and Merlyn were concerned about their other sons who were into the party scene, as well as their marital problems. News of the death of long-time-friend, Roger Maris, was a crushing blow for Mantle. There seemed to be no end to the tragedies that struck the family. Merlyn believed that her husband took the casino job because of Billy's mounting medical bills. Mickey said later, "I acted like it didn't bother me but it did" (Agape Press). By March of 1985, Mickey was happy to hear that Peter Ueberroff, baseball's new MLB commissioner, had rescinded Kuhn's decision against Mickey's involvement with the casino.

Finally there was a ray of sunshine in his life. The Hall of Fame inductee found that his years of popularity were best matched with the growing baseball collectables business. Mickey started making appearances around the country as a guest speaker, as well as making himself available to sign autographs and sell sports collectible merchandise. Mickey's popularity was so great that he hired a staff to organize and invite some of his old baseball buddies to speak at events with him.

Mantle's absences from home continued to wear on his wife, Merlyn. The arguing, the fights and the tragedies had taken their toll. By the late '80s Merlyn and Mickey separated. It was a difficult time for them both. Mickey's old friend and baseball room-mate, Billy Martin, died in 1989 in a car accident. This was devastating to Mickey. The emotional turmoil was building. Somehow Merlyn, found the strength to get help with her alcohol problems through the Twelve-Step program. It appeared that Merlyn's religious family roots helped her overcome her addiction. Gradually others in her family followed her lead in getting help as well.

There was another special person in Mantle's life. In the 1950s Mantle used the same locker stall as another New York professional athlete, Pat Summerall, but during different seasons. Summerall recalled that he first met Mantle when they played minor league baseball together. Over the years Summerall and Mantle played a lot of golf and interacted socially, the NFL announcer would recall in 2005. [30]

After Mantle's friend, Pat Summerall entered the Betty Ford Center for Alcohol in the early 1990's, Mickey showed interest in getting help. Summerall later shared, "Mickey was concerned about his alcohol consumption." [31] After many long question-and-answer sessions with his friend, Pat challenged Mantle to enter the clinic. "Mickey agreed to enter the facility, and did so on a day not normally reserved for new patients." [32]

Perhaps this was the most difficult decision of his life. One can only wonder what if this choice had been made years earlier. "It was the policy of the Betty Ford Center to disallow outgoing telephone calls during a patient's one month stay. Summerall fondly remembers how Mantle somehow got on the phone and called his friend a number of times, sometimes late at night. While this was a tough time in Mickey's life, both Richardson and Summerall agree their friend was later to become an outstanding spokesman for people everywhere who were suffering from alcoholism." [33]

The Mantle family was struck with sadness and tragedy again when their thirty-six year old son, Billy, died of Hodgkin's disease that March. Within a number of weeks Mickey did something that other reformed alcoholics would come to admire. On a front cover story of Sport's Illustrated, Mickey disclosed the story of his struggle with alcohol. As Mickey exposed the destructive nature of alcohol abuse, his cover story allowed millions of people to better understand the negative consequences of alcoholism. Mantle's courageous magazine testimony in 1994 shed light on an issue that many people needed to hear.

By 1995, Mantle's health took a turn for the worse when it was discovered he had cancer – as well as liver problems. While hospitalized, Mantle called his old teammate and friend, Bobby Richardson, and asked him to pray for him. Richardson vividly remembers visiting Mantle a few weeks before his death on August 13, 1995. One of the first things that Mantle wanted to tell his former teammate was that he now trusted in Christ as his Lord and Savior.[34]

With the help of wonderful friends such as Bobby Richardson and Pat Summerall, Mantle went from being a hell raiser off the field to being raised into heaven. "Years later Richardson found out that Mantle, while in the hospital, somehow listened to a Focus on the Family testimonial tape of NBA Hall of Famer, Pete Maravich. Commenting on how Pete Maravich's testimony was instrumental in leading Mantle to Christ, focus Vice President Kurt Bruner explained "after achieving nearly everything that the world has to offer and finding that something was still lacking, Pete (Maravich) discovered Jesus Christ and never looked back."[35]

When Mickey Mantle hit a home run he didn't need to follow the ball into the bleachers because he knew he had hit the it out of the park. It was the same with his spiritual life. Once Mickey accepted Christ he never looked back at his past or his sin. He had hit a home run with God: into the record book—the Book of Life.

Chapter 2

George Washington: The Untold Story

O ne has to wonder what goes into the making of a president. What influences and molds a future president and exactly what kind of man volunteers to shoulder the responsibility of an entire nation? George Washington, a man with humble beginnings, was able to help shape this country because of what first shaped his heart and mind.

Bridges Creek added to its census the only president ever to be born there on February 22, 1732. The rich farmlands of Westmoreland County, Virginia were called home by George and his seven younger siblings. His father, Augustus (Augustine) Washington, had lost his first wife but did not waste any time trying to raise his four children alone. He quickly took a second wife, Mary Ball, George's mother. The children lacked for nothing as Augustus was considered a prosperous landholder, with Mary wealthy in her own right.

Washington had a practical, though sporadic, education at home where he learned arithmetic, grammar, geography, geometry and trigonometry. He showed great skill and interest in map reading which came in handy for the management of the family's large parcels of land.

After many years of good eating, his forty-nine year old father died from stomach gout on April 12, 1743 when George was only eleven. Augustus Washington's will divided his land holdings amongst his sons. George's inheritance included sharing five thousand acres with two of his brothers as well as three lots in Fredericksburg, Virginia. His half brothers, Lawrence and Austin, helped Washington manage his inheritance. His stepbrother, Lawrence, inherited a land parcel along the Potomac which later became known as the beautiful Mt. Vernon.

Washington acquired a fascination for the art of surveying. When his stepbrother, Lawrence, married into the wealthy Fairfax family, the door was opened for George to further develop his skills as a young surveyor. George took a surveying course (1745-1746), and learned to draft and map surveys of properties. Washington's propensity for mathematics came into play as well. When his stepbrother Lawrence died of tuberculosis in 1751, George discovered that he suddenly owned substantial land holdings including the estate with the parcel in Mt. Vernon.

The Fairfax family hired him as an assistant to a professional surveyor and assigned the task of surveying Fairfax's extensive land holdings in Northern Virginia and the beautiful Shenandoah Valley. While surveying the Fairfax estate that spanned from the Potomac to the western parts of the Alleghenies, Washington encountered his first Indians. The young man began to formulate ideas about how the colonies could explore new territories west of Virginia. Although he was only seventeen, on July 20, 1749, he was appointed as the surveyor for Culpepper County, Virginia.

Washington shared many of the religious beliefs of his fellow Virginians. He was baptized in the Church of England but faithfully attended the Episcopal Church. According to the Britannica, Washington was an active member and later vestryman of the Episcopal Church.

In his early twenties Washington decided to join the Free Masons. He had limited participation with the Masons, with Masonic authority William Adrian Brown identifying only twenty-nine activities involving Washington [36] during his lifetime. Masonic lodges in the military were generally recognized as social meeting places for troops who were away from home. (Historical accounts confirm this). George tried to live a life of godly principles and decided that joining the Masons could only benefit him. During the 1700s, early American lodges openly promoted Christian principles and ministries.[37] Freemasons were required to practice Christian orthodox principles and George Washington believed he was in good company.

Washington's Military Exploits

England had firmly established its control over the east coast by 1750, while France began to challenge England's control over the regions of the west, far south and far north. France exerted influence and control over Montreal, Canada, the Ohio River valley and Louisiana. The storm was on the horizon.

The unrest in the colonies turned Washington's attention toward the military in 1752 and he was appointed major of the Virginia militia. George's surveying exploits in the west had served him well. The thin-faced, blue-eyed twenty-year-old must have made a distinct impression on Virginia's Governor Robert Dinwiddie who entrusted him to deliver an ultimatum to the French demanding they stop their expansion and development in the Ohio frontier. The governor also sent Washington to meet with the English and advise them to stop their interference of English colonists traveling west into the Ohio River frontier. However, the French subsequently ignored Gov. Dinwiddie's plea and it became apparent that the French were a threat to Virginia. Washington was promoted to the rank of lieutenant colonel in the Virginia militia during the next year.

The governor sent an expeditionary team led by the twenty-two year old Washington to remove the French from around Fort Duquesne. At Fort Necessity, militia troops were soundly beaten and driven back. Washington was then appointed as an aide to British General Edward Braddock who met with colonial governors to discuss the military campaign against the French intruders in April of 1755. Washington's mother met with him as well, expressing her concern for his safety. His response was endearing. "The God, to whom you commended me, madam, when I set out upon a more perilous errand, defended me from all harm, and I trust He will do so now."[38]

Benjamin Franklin warned the English general about the guerrilla tactics used by the French and their Indian allies. The Indians were stealth, under-cover fighters who lay camouflaged ambushes for their enemies. Braddock did not heed Franklin which would later result in many deaths, including his own.

The war was on. In the summer of 1755, red-uniformed British soldiers moved west, marching in slender military column following the trails to Fort Duquesne. The British were confident that the French and Indians were not only fewer in number, but militarily inferior. Even Washington tried to persuade Braddock to send Indian scouts, but the hard-headed British general ignored him. He remained convinced that his seasoned militia would see victory.

Braddock and a combined force of over 2,000 men (consisting primarily of British soldiers, a few colonists and one aide-de-camp, George Washington) headed west for Fort Duquesne to remove the French from their land. Two months later, (July 9, 1755), Braddock and his troops were camped near the French outpost. The combined forces of 855 French, Canadians and Indians overtook the 1300 British regulars about seven miles from the fort. The Indians comprised most of the expedition and, just as Franklin and Washington had warned, the under-cover ambush known as the Battle of Monongahela greatly wounded the British.

The soldiers began to panic. The Indians and their French allies quickly seized on the vulnerability of the British as their camouflaged forces pinned down and surrounded them. Their forces were picked off one at a time, their bright red uniforms making them easy targets. The Indians had been instructed to take out the officers. Tragically, 714 soldiers lost their lives along with General Braddock. Washington survived the slaughter but it was a crushing blow for the British and their colonial allies.

Fifteen years later, while exploring land near the junction of the Ohio and Kanawha Rivers, George Washington met the same Chief Red Hawk who had faced him in that famous battle. The chief addressed Washington as follows: "I am a chief and ruler over tribes. My influence extends to the waters of the great lakes and to the far Blue Mountains. I have traveled a long and weary path that I might see the young warrior of the great battle. It was on a day when the white man's blood mixed with the streams of our forest that I first beheld this Chief (Washington) ... Our rifles were leveled, rifles which, but for you, knew not how to miss – 'twas all in vain; a power mightier far than we shielded you. Seeing you were under the special guardianship of the Great Spirit, we immediately ceased to fire on you...I am come to pay homage to the man who is the particular favorite of Heaven and who can never die in battle." [39]

The testimony of Mary Draper Ingels from Draper Meadows, Virginia confirms this exchange. She had been captured and held for two months by Shawnee Indians in 1755. While in the Indian camp, she recalled hearing several Frenchmen discussing Red Hawk's attempt to shoot at Washington eleven different times, deciding to finally stop when the chief became "convinced that the Great Spirit protected him (Washington)." [40]

It soon became apparent to the Virginia Regiment commanders that Washington's military leadership skills made him a vital asset to their efforts. Washington was promoted by his superiors to colonel that August and was subsequently put in charge of all Virginia operations. Under his command, Fort Duquesne was brought down in 1758 and a settlement (Pittsburgh) was established.

Entering Politics and the Issue of Slavery

Washington next entered the political arena. On July 24, 1758 the twenty-seven year old colonel was elected burgess of Frederick County, Virginia. He resigned his military commission and on January 6, 1759 he married widow Martha Dandridge Curtis. Martha brought substantial assets and her two children, Jackie and Patsy, into the marriage. Due to health problems, they never had children of their own. Her assets helped George pay off his debts as well as assisted him in meeting the demanding financial needs of the family's farm.

Washington became more involved in the everyday operation of the land he had inherited from his father Augustine and stepbrother Lawrence. Land owners needed cheap help to produce a labor intensive crop like tobacco. The labor requirements of raising tobacco forced many land owners to consider planting other types of crops such as wheat, corn, potatoes and peas. Farmers often used labor from new immigrants to work off their traveling debts.

The Dutch introduced the slave trade in the early 1600s. African chieftains sold their own people to Portuguese traders who in turn brought them to the colonies. The slave trade was unacceptable to many Christians in the colonies but their minority opposition was not strong enough to overturn its practice.

Washington initially followed the majority and not only tolerated the slave trade but benefited from it. However he did believe that slave families under his care should never be separated or mistreated. His slaves were educated, baptized and taken care of in their old age. During Washington's later years, he grew more uneasy with slavery. George Washington eventually came to believe that slavery was morally repugnant. Late in his life the first president made provisions to free his slaves upon his and Martha's death.

Washington and other land owners became discontent with British colonial rule and tobacco traders. The system of debt and trade (with English traders) offered them little economic benefit. It preserved a system that promoted cheap labor, (slavery), and one that clearly favored the English traders. Many colonial farmers were regularly in debt to their British trading partners and their resentment grew each season. Washington gradually changed his estate's dependence from tobacco to wheat and added horse breeding, flour milling, weaving and fishing to generate revenue. This diversity allowed Mt. Vernon to become a self-sufficient operation.

Washington entered public service in his early thirties. His stellar military performance in the French and Indian campaign together with his participation in the House of Burgess' caused his reputation to flourish. He was exasperated with English rule and considered the new colonial taxes to be an invasion of Virginia's rights and liberties. He took part in a boycott of English goods until Parliament decided to rescind the burdensome new tax. A new royal decree mandated in London by King George III limited all colonists' land ownership rights to territories west of the Appalachian Mountains.

Frustration was mounting in the hearts and minds of other colonial leaders up and down the Atlantic seaboard. Washington tried to maintain a positive attitude and hoped that England would compromise on their position. They did not, and the conflict escalated. The Stamp Act of1765, the Townsend Revenue Act in 1767 and finally the Tea Act (1773), created a climate of hostility toward the monarchy that spread throughout the colonies. The colonists became increasingly irritated by England's denial of representation. [41] Contention exploded into violence at the Boston Massacre and Lexington and Concord. In July 1774, Washington participated in The Fairfax Resolves calling for a meeting of a Continental Congress which included representatives from all thirteen colonies.

Declaring Independence

The colonists were motivated by frustration and rage; the British with greed. The mix was volatile. The First Continental Congress in Philadelphia convened a few months later in September. Washington was appointed as a delegate from the state of Virginia. The foundation for change was being laid; and by May of 1775, a Second Continental Congress convened. Congress created the Continental Army in June and George Washington was appointed its commander. The colonists were to reject Britain's monarchy and the British Parliament.

The British were highly visible and maintained military superiority over the east coast, however they experienced difficulty controlling the interior portions of the colonies. By March of 1776, the Continental Army occupied Boston. The Continental Congress convened in Philadelphia from July 1-4, 1776 to debate the merits of their Declaration of Independence. On July 4th the Declaration of Independence was signed by fifty-six signors. By affixing their names to the document, they forfeited their welfare and personal safety. Freedom lay just ahead but lives would be lost in the process.

All of the fifty-six signors of the Declaration of Independence, except two, were members of Christian churches, which included the Anglican, Congregational, Episcopalian, Presbyterian, Catholic and Unitarian denominations. (The future president was a member of the Pohick Church in Virginia.) [42] Additionally, four of the signors were current or full time ministers. In 1848, author B.J. Loosing wrote that the signors were "instruments of providence" who recognized that the teachings of the Bible had a strong influence in the creation of this historical document. God's influence was profound.

Washington knew that liberty would not be without cost. The general made sure that someone read the Declaration of Independence to his fledgling Army regulars upon arrival in New York.

While the British defeated General Washington's forces in the Battle of Long Island that August, it did not yet dampen the spirits of the freedom fighters. Washington and his outmanned regulars experienced unbearable hardships and by the next month the British were occupying New York City. The losses mounted and things were not looking good for Washington. He desperately needed a victory to renew morale within his ranks. He found it in Trenton. [43]

On December 25, 1776 Washington crossed the partially frozen Delaware River in the dark with 2400 soldiers. The Hessians were totally unprepared and were overtaken on December 26, 1776. [44] The surprise and subsequent victory over the English was an important and much needed victory for the Americans. That winning battle along with the successfully led invasion and victory at Princeton, New Jersey, on January 3, 1777 delivered munitions to the general's beleaguered forces.

But most importantly these events bolstered the spirits of not only the Continental Army but also the newly created Continental Congress and the colonists supporting the war. The victories "brought recruits flocking to camp in the spring and encouraged foreign sympathizers with the American cause." [45]

Every war puts financial stress on the supporters, and even army regulars often went unpaid. Washington had a difficult time getting blankets and tents for his soldiers and sometimes used his own finances for the army's basic necessities. Finally the French started contributing supplies and money after hearing of Washington's two victories. Washington decided to reorganize his army and reward men for re-enlisting while punishing those who deserted.

Fortunately for the Americans the British did not press the Continental Army during the harsh winter months of 1777. That winter and up to the beginning of the spring of 1778, Washington and his troops encamped at Valley Forge, Pennsylvania, in tents as this was before log hut barracks were built. "When complete, each dirt-floor hut measured about fourteen by sixteen feet. In spite of the small size, about twelve soldiers lived in each hut." [46] The winter took its toll on the 12,000 troops with over a quarter of them perishing from cold or disease. During the spring, the tattered and ill-equipped soldiers were trained by Baron Von Steuben, a friend of Benjamin Franklin. The Prussian military veteran became their expert drill instructor during this critical period in 1778. Washington, in his own words, "viewed him in the light of the good officer," [47] and the baron was later assigned to the rank of general in Washington's army.

Washington wisely surrounded himself with skilled commanders (i.e. Alexander Hamilton, Horatio Gates, Robert Howe, Marquis de Lafayette, William Alexander, Nathanael Greene, and John Paul Jones to name a few). Completely dedicated to their commanding general, they served their leader well.

Washington felt that the Americans were ill equipped to fight a short, intensive war against the seasoned British. He remained convinced that the key to winning the war was to outlast them. With no definitive plan, Washington realized that the struggle for freedom rested divinely in the hands of God. In his September 1780 address to his troops Washington wrote, "The Providential train of circumstances which led to it affords the most convincing proof that the liberties of America are the object of Divine Protection." [48]

As each year passed, there were few bright spots in the colony's struggle for freedom. In most of their encounters with the British, the Continental Army was beaten in every single battle by their more experienced opponent. All that changed when France decided, (with the urging of Franklin and Lafayette), to ally themselves with the Americans. Initially Washington was reluctant to join the forces together; however, when the British scored two more major battles, he knew it was time to accept this ally.

France had a seasoned and reliable navy and even with the ongoing mitigating differences of opinion about land exploration, the Continental Army desperately needed their support.

General Cornwallis commanded a large British military base located along the Chesapeake which was particularly vulnerable to attack because they did not have good naval support. French Admiral de Grasse sailed an armada of twenty-eight ships that contributed to the efforts of the colonist and French troops. Some 16,500 troops came together to attack Cornwallis' position from land and sea at Yorktown ending with a humiliating surrender on October 19, 1781. It was a great victory for the united forces. On November 30, 1782 the British and the Americans signed a preliminary Article of Peace. By September 3rd of the following year, the Americans and the British signed the Treaty of Paris, thus recognizing the independence of the United States of America.

Life for Washington after the Revolutionary War

Washington had dedicated eight long years of his life to the war effort and resigned as commander of the Continental Army on December 23, 1783. During the years of war, Washington had not been able to attend to his home at Mt. Vernon. Martha went to meet him on several occasions, but Washington had sacrificed much of his personal life to lead the new nation during war.

When Washington returned to Mt. Vernon in 1783, he found his beloved home in a rundown condition. As Washington lent his attention to the neglected affairs of his Mt. Vernon estate, he became increasingly concerned about the vulnerability of the fragile young country. This helped persuade him to participate in the Constitution Convention in Philadelphia in May of 1787.

The representatives unanimously elected him President of the Convention. There were a number of drafts and proposals put forth by the delegates. Each state had to ratify the document but by September of 1787, the convention signed off on the draft of the new constitution which essentially provided the framework for the creation and formation of the United States federal government. The intention was to balance power and influence between the three branches of the new government. The document was approved and ratified by the majority of states. In a public statement issued in 1789, Washington thanked "the great Lord and ruler of Nations" for enabling us "to establish constitutions of government for our safety and happiness, and particularly the national one now lately instituted." He went on by saying that it is "the duty of all nations to acknowledge the providence of Almighty God, to obey his will, to be grateful for all his benefits." [49] Certainly, Washington recognized God's divine hand in the creation of his new country. While he realized America's future was fragile, he also understood that God's hand was providentially involved in the formation of the country.

The respect that Washington garnered from his peers made him the most likely choice as President. George Washington was unanimously elected president of the United States (by his Convention peers) on February 4, 1789. George Washington would once again relinquish his private life for service to his country. Sworn in as president at the Federal Hall in New York City on April 30, 1789, at the age of fifty-seven, he took the inaugural oath. Washington issued the new country's first Thanksgiving proclamation when he assigned Thursday, November 26th as a day to give thanks. In his proclamation Washington asked that the nation unite in "humbly offering our prayers and supplications to the great Lord and Ruler of the Nations and beseech Him to pardon our national and other transgressions ...."[50]

The Washington family moved to Philadelphia. There he appointed some remarkable men to the executive branch's first cabinet. Thomas Jefferson became the first Secretary of State. Alexander Hamilton became the Secretary of Treasury and John Adams, a devout Christian, was Washington's vice president. John Jay, another strong believer in Christ, was nominated as the nation's first Supreme Court Chief Justice. Finally they were one nation under God.

President Washington attended the Episcopal Church regularly when he stayed in New York and the Christ Church when in Philadelphia. As an effective chief executive, Washington depended heavily on his cabinet to direct the new country. During his first term, fellow Virginian James Madison began writing and developing the first ten amendments of the U.S. Constitution. These amendments became instrumental in upholding the freedom and liberty of Americans and new citizens and all ten were ratified by Dec. 15, 1791 before Washington's first term expired.

Washington's presidency was marked by a number of notable highlights. Realizing the fragility of the new nation, Washington decided it was in America's best interest to remain neutral in foreign affairs. Wisely, he wouldn't commit his country's allegiance to any one foreign power. Later in life, Washington was to become one of the more outspoken advocates against slavery and on May 13, 1787 said that it was "among my first wishes to see some plan adopted by which slavery in this country may be abolished by slow, sure and imperceptible degrees." [51] Unfortunately, his efforts to do so were in vain considering the strong opposition he found from the farm states. Washington realized that the country was too young and fragile for the system to change at that time. He wrote in 1786, "There is not a man living who wishes more sincerely than I do, to see a plan adopted for the abolition of slavery." [52]

During his second term as president, it became clear that the country needed to mend its foreign relations. John Jay helped develop a plan to normalize relations with their former war opponent, Great Britain. The British and the Americans signed a treaty wherein the British agreed to forgive pre-Revolutionary war debt, abandon their forts along the Great Lakes, and open their economic trade to the Americans.

As George Washington's second term neared an end, it became evident that his propensity for prayer and following Almighty God had become foundational to his success as a leader. The first president's sincerity and reverence towards God were noteworthy. One friend and former military associate, John Marshall (later appointed Chief Justice of the Supreme Court) observed, "Washington was a sincere believer in the Christian faith." J.M. Sewell, a poet, also described his friend Washington as a firm believer in the Christian religion. [53] J. Smith, a soldier in the colonial war and another congressman while Washington was president said, "George Washington was neither ostentatious nor ashamed of his Christian profession." [54] Other congressmen also confirmed this. Washington's pastor from his Virginia church declared the president "was a professor of Christianity." [55]

Perhaps the most powerful testament to Washington's dedication to his Christian faith came from his own adopted daughter,

Nelly Custis Lewis. She said that while living in the city (in both Philadelphia and New York during his days as president), her father attended church regularly. Nelly was particularly touched when she witnessed her adopted father praying fervently for a sick aunt. "In a letter she wrote to Jared Sparks, a Chaplain of Congress, Nelly forcefully declared: I should have thought it the greatest heresy to doubt his firm belief in Christianity...."[56]

In Washington's farewell speech delivered on September 17, 1796, he reminded all Americans "of all the dispositions and habits which lead to political prosperity, religion and morality are indispensable supports."[57] Washington understood the importance that Christianity played in the formation of the new nation. In an earlier letter to Brigadier General Nelson (referring to the founding of the country), Washington stated that "the hand of Providence has been so conspicuous in all this that he must be worse than an infidel that lacks faith, and more than wicked, that has not gratitude enough to acknowledge his obligations."[58]

George Washington retired to his beloved Mt. Vernon in March of 1797 after his successor's inauguration. He lived only two and a half more years after he left public office. He succumbed to pneumonia and acute laryngitis.

In his many official orders and writings to his troops as Army Commander-in-Chief, Washington expressed that every soldier would "endeavor so to love and act as becomes a Christian soldier." Near death he told his doctor, "I have no fear, Doctor, to die."[59] Nelly, Washington's adopted daughter also confirmed the story of her father's death. She explained how Martha simply "resigned (George) without murmur, into the arms of his Savior and God, with the assured hope of his eternal happiness in Heaven."[60]

A personalized well-worn prayer book was found among the former president's belongings. Clearly God's hand was on this famous founding father of our nation. Washington's deep faith in God was pivotal in the founding of our country. He used his faith as the key to open the door to a life that was to play a vital role in the birth of America.

Chapter 3

Steve McQueen Hollywood's "King of Cool"

Times change and time changes everything! What did the America look like when Steve McQueen entered the world on March 24, 1930? Well, bread cost $.09, a gallon of gasoline cost $.10 and a new home cost a little over $7,000. Clarence Birdseye introduced frozen food to the country. John Dillinger made an escape from prison using a wooden rifle. It was also during that year that Hollywood introduced the viewer guide ratings required by the motion picture industry.

William McQueen, Steve's dad, flew off to find his fame and fortune as a circus stunt pilot when Steve was just six months old. Unfortunately, his mother, Julia (aka Jullian) Crawford, turned to alcohol to cope with her problems, and so Steve was sent to live with his uncle, Claude Thomson. Claude was a prosperous pig farmer in Slater, Illinois. McQueen recalled his years with Claude as a happy and innocent time as he enjoyed the simple farm life in Slater. Being too young to understand what had happened, Steve "began fantasizing about where (his mother) might be and what she was doing."[61]

That question was soon answered when Jullian came back into Steve's life. She had remarried and deceided that Steve should come to live them in Indianapolis, Indiana. Leaving the farm was difficult, as Steve had grown attached to Claude and regarded him as a father figure.

The plan ultimately backfired when Steve found he could not adjust to living with Jullian and her new husband. He spent more and more time on the streets, and his life on Uncle Claude's farm seemed far away. When Steve started getting into trouble with gangs, Jullian again sought help from Claude, and Steve returned to the farm for three more years.

History repeated itself when his mother removed him from the farm again, this time to live in LA with yet another new stepfather. Again Steve rebelled against the change but this time physical violence erupted. Jullian continued her drinking, and Steve returned to Uncle Claude for a third time. However, this time was different because Steve had grown accustomed to his independence. He became fascinated with the circus and was again lured away from Claude.

McQueen eventually wandered back to Los Angeles where his mother was still living and sought refuge in the streets. His relationship with Berri, his newest stepfather, became intolerable as Steve received a beating each time he got into trouble. During a knockdown, drag-out fight, the young McQueen threatened to kill Berri. Berri pressured Jullian into signing a court order stating that Steve was incorrigible. The order ultimately wound up with Steve being sent to the Boy's Republic in Chino, CA. [62]

At first, Steve wanted nothing to do with learning the philosophical principles of the Boy's Republic that included "accountability, earning self-esteem through personal accomplishment, group involvement and nothing without labor." [63] Troubled boys who entered the program were taught that their progress depended on their attitude and willingness to make changes and improvements.

Steve had some initial adjustment problems in relating to the structure. Years later, McQueen attributed his turn around to friend and advisor, Mr. Panter. This man reminded Steve of Uncle Claude as he took a personal interest in him. Things were starting to look up for Steve and he began to thrive under the tutelage of Panter. He began to learn some of the valuable concepts of the program. McQueen later stated, "The Boy's Republic saved my life," [64] Steve demonstrated his gratitude to the program by generously donating a building on their campus that is still there today.

Steve's mother visited him at The Boy's Republic to inform him that his stepfather had died. His mother was now living in New York with a new boyfriend, and she wanted Steve to join her in Greenwich Village. Jullian actually wanted Steve to live downstairs with a gay roommate. He complied but it didn't take long for Steve to feel uncomfortable with his accommodations. He went into survival mode and began drifting. At seventeen, McQueen enlisted in the Marines. Although he had problems with authority, Steve ultimately dedicated himself to the task of completing his U.S. military service and received an honorable discharge in 1950.

After stumbling through a variety of jobs, Steve decided to take advantage of some of the benefits afforded him by his military service and used the GI bill to secure additional schooling at New York's neighborhood playhouse. Convincing the school to accept him, Steve's competitive nature and personal drive helped him land a scholarship with the Hebert Bergoff Drama School. Steve's participation with the school started paying off as he started receiving acting jobs around the Big Apple. He procured a role in the Broadway play, A Hatful of Rain (starring Ben Gazzara) which led the young actor to other opportunities in the profession. [65]

In his spare time, McQueen found time for a sport he absolutely loved, racing motorcycles at the Long Island Raceway.

In 1956, McQueen met his future wife, Neile Adams, who was planning to be a professional dancer. She had obtained a scholarship with the talented dance instructor, Katherine Dunham. Steve and Neile lived together in her New York apartment. Neile was also a promising actress and was cast in the highly successful play, The Pajama Game. It was also around this time that Neile got a call from movie industry representatives for an upcoming screen test in California. After her screen test, Neile asked Steve to join her in Hollywood. Initially he refused, but three days later he joined her. Although McQueen had made it clear he was not the marrying kind, in November 2, 1956 the young couple were officially married. [66]

His wife achieved over twenty appearances in both film and television and was an accomplished, talented actress and dancer. Her contacts helped establish Steve in his career.[67] Finally it seemed that McQueen had found himself an occupation where he could excel, although initially Neile's agent Hilly Elkins didn't think much of McQueen's acting abilities. Nevertheless Neile persuaded Hilly to help her husband find some work. Steve appeared on TV for the first time in The Defenders.

Again, with the help of Elkins, Steve landed another role in the movie, Somebody Up There Likes Me. Steve played a minor role, but it provided a break the young actor needed. It became evident that Steve desired to succeed in this very competitive business. Since he wasn't familiar with acting on the big screen, Elkins thought he could find the actor some work in lower tier movies. In September of 1958, McQueen procured the starring teenage role in the hugely successful cult movie, The Blob. Still not satisfied, McQueen wanted more.

At the time, television was a brand new venue with its potential not yet realized. Hilly Elkins felt that his client could do well in the role as the young bounty hunter in a new TV pilot, Wanted: Dead or Alive. This program aired in the fall of 1958 and was subsequently picked up by the CBS television network. McQueen's leading role provided steady income and allowed the young actor to hon his acting skills. The thirty-minute TV show also proved to be popular with the television audience that first year and ranked in the top ten. Notable stars appeared on the series including Michael Landon (of Bonanza and Little House on the Prairie fame), DeForest Kelly (later a star in the wildly popular Star Trek series), and James Coburn.[68]

McQueen's big break came during the late '50s at the expense of a frayed relationship between Frank Sinatra and Sammy Davis Jr. Sinatra and fellow "Rat Pack" member, Sammy Davis Jr., were slated to be in the film. The famous singer, Sinatra, had a short falling out with Davis prior to filming which opened the other leading role. Never So Few was released in December of 1959 and McQueen made the most of his role. Variety Magazine took note saying the actor "delivers with impressive style."

In Sturges' 1960 film, The Magnificent Seven, Steve finally got an opportunity to show off his acting ability and earned a prominent position in the movie's marquee.[69]

Steve and Neile had roles off screen as well. A daughter, Terry, (born 6/5/59) and a son, Chad, (born 12/28/60) took much of the couple's time and attention.

McQueen's weekly program, Wanted: Dead or Alive was cancelled in 1961, but he was busier than ever with upcoming movie projects. The Great Escape boosted McQueen to world-wide fame; having all the ingredients of a truly great movie. The film became well known for the exciting motorcycle scenes that featured McQueen and his stunt driver, Bud Elkins. The film boasted names such as Richard Attenborough, Donald Pleasence and James Garner, Steve's future neighbor.

Steve's celebrity made him popular with the women as well. Hollywood became his playground and his multiple affairs were described in various gossip magazines. His friends even attested to that fact and that he also had a reputation of being difficult to deal with on the movie set. (Although his friends witnessed his softer side when he received the news of his mother's death in 1965).

Steve began to take on more interesting roles. He starred in a number of different movies over the next few years. They included Love with the Proper Stranger (December, 1963) with co-star Natalie Wood, Baby the Rain Must Fall (January, 1965), the Cincinnati Kid (October, 1965), Nevada Smith (June, 1966) and The Sand Pebbles (December, 1966). McQueen also earned a Best Actor academy award nomination for his acting ability in the film The Sand Pebbles.[70]

The late '60s brought about a time of tremendous social, political and cultural turmoil. According to author Marshall Terrill's book, Steve McQueen – Portrait of an American Rebel, Neile McQueen admitted her husband's lifestyle during this time helped to undermine their marriage.[71] Some of Steve's Hollywood connections had an impact on the star and his relationship with his wife, as the movie industry has a tendency to mock traditional values.

Steve's most notable films were released in the late '60s of which The Thomas Crown Affair shot to the top of the list. While fans proclaimed Bullitt the best, this movie brought about a new relation-ship between Robert Vaughn and the cool McQueen; one that would last for the rest of his life.

The actor also participated in the documentary, On Any Given Sunday, a film about motorcycle racing. Financially, On Any Given Sunday grossed more than $25 million world-wide. The now- famous actor was even featured riding a dirt bike on the front cover of Sports Illustrated (8/23/71).

The '70s saw also some notable changes in the forty-year old actor's life, including his marriage. His affairs had hurt his wife irreparably. In an interview many years later, James Garner referred to Steve as wild and crazy. Some speculated that a mid-life crisis of sorts caused him to wander. Regardless, he continued to show devo-tion to his children. Neile struggled with his behavior and could not overlook his indiscrestions.

Neile's divorce from Steve became official in March 1972, thus ending their fifteen year marriage. In her book, My Husband, My Friend, Neile said her relationship with Steve seemed more like a partnership. Her book tells of "a Steve McQueen no one knew, his good side, his crazy side, his dark side." [72]

For several years, McQueen hoped to repeat the film success he had with his 1968 blockbuster, Bullit. Disappointment set in 1972 when his film about a rodeo rider, Junior Bonner, did poorly at the box office but was quickly replaced with the success of The Getaway. Directed by Sam Peckinpah, it featured McQueen and Ali McGraw. Just a year earlier she had starred in a blockbuster success that had been nominated for seven academy awards. McGraw played the role of lead character, Jennifer Cavelleri, in Love Story.

The Getaway, laced with a series of action sequences including car chases, gun battles, fight scenes and shoot-outs, brought life to the screen. In the virtual audio commentary of the film (provided by Warner Brothers Entertainment), Peckinpah said the film showed the ups and downs of the human relationship between McCoy and his wife Carol, (played by McQueen and McGraw). Warner Brothers quoted McQueen who said that the chemistry of the couple in the film portrayed an honest relationship between them. In the same

Warner Brothers audio commentary, McGraw admitted that she had the utmost respect for the forty-two year old McQueen, but that she was "terrified working across the camera from him."[73]

The Getaway was a huge success grossing over thirty-five million dollars. On the set rumors sprouted about a reported romantic affair between McQueen and the younger actress. As it turned out, McGraw's romantic relationship with McQueen ended her marriage to her then husband and movie executive, Robert Evans. Ironically, it had been Evans who helped procure his wife the co-starring role. Hollywood gossip buzzed about McQueen's relationship with McGraw.

By the summer of 1973, the couple married. The actor's professional success continued with the release of the highly acclaimed film, Papillon. A number of film critics considered Steve's role as prisoner, Henri 'Papillon' Charriere, in the French penal colony, one of his best. His co-star, Dustin Hoffman, already had some notable works to his credit, including the Graduate (1967) and Midnight Cowboy (1969).

McQueen, along with actor Paul Newman, shared leading roles in the disaster film, Towering Inferno in 1974. The movie plot centered around a disastrous fire that took place in a tall San Francisco skyscraper and the drama that surrounded the fire. The film was loaded with stars including William Holden, Faye Dunaway and Fred Astaire.[74]

Steve McQueen had climbed to the top and it seemed as if there were no more mountains to climb. The actor had made millions; far exceeding anyone's expectations. He had two young children who he loved and a cordial relationship with their mother, Neile.

He also had a new love in his life. Ali McGraw sacrificed for her new marriage with Steve by temporarily giving up her promising acting and modeling career. McQueen's career, however, turned a corner and it seemed that the forty-five year old actor had lost interest in producing the regular block-buster hits his fans had come to expect. Steve's interest in the acting profession waned. His personal life had become tumultuous. According to Hollywood reporter, Steve Hulver, the actor "delved ... into a dark ... Hollywood scene filled with drink, drugs and womanizing."

Given the new road that McQueen seemed to be traveling, it appeared that his relationship with Ali MacGraw was deteriorating. As author, Marshall Terrill wrote in his well documented book on the actor's life, Steve McQueen – Portrait of an American Rebel, that Steve's indulgence with alcohol and pot concerned his wife. It seemed that a black abyss of depression began to control his life and he simply was not coping well. [75]

With the film The Enemy of the People, McQueen made a movie as part of a contractual commitment he had to fulfill to the studio. The movie, based on a play by Henrik Ibsen; cast the story of Dr. Thomas Stockmann. The movie was never officially released by the studio, but did contain an interesting line the actor declared in one scene, "Was the majority right when the people stood by when they crucified Jesus?"

Still Steve and Ali struggled. Years later MacGraw recounts in her book, Moving Pictures, her tumultuous relationship with McQueen, It was difficult for those close to him, especially his wife, to deal with the actor's penchant for alcohol and other stimulants. Just as he had in his previous marriage with Neile, the forty-seven-year old actor had the reputation of having a wandering eye and by 1978 divorce ended the couple's five-year marriage.

From the mid to late 1970s his appearance changed and morphed into someone more like a mountain man than the millionaire actor of world-wide fame. During this time Steve went to great lengths to protect his privacy. In author Grady Ragsdale's book, Steve McQueen, the Final Chapter, the author wrote that Steve was "an American original, a tough guy with a troubled past who touches the rebel in each of us. He tended to be a loner, quiet and introspective." [76] His early years hadn't completely left him; the accomplished actor was still searching for something he hadn't found. That was about to change.

Steve McQueen was his own man. He loved wearing blue jeans, riding dirt bikes, hanging out with his teenage children, but deep inside his heart, something was missing. He also had a new girl friend; college student and model, Barbara Minty. In 1977, Steve spotted his future girl friend "in a Club Med advertisement while he was on the airplane and wanted (her) to audition for a part in his new movie." [77] Barbara Minty had been featured on the front cover of Look – Hawaii magazine and her modeling career blossomed. Intrigued by her beauty and personality, McQueen was smitten. Soon Steve created the opportunity to introduce himself to Barbara.

It was during that decade that Minty was featured on the cover of a number of high profile magazines including Glamour, Elle, and Cosmopolitan. As a professional model, she did quite a bit of national advertising besides being featured in Harper's Bazaar and Sports Illustrated. Minty was also handy with a camera. (Her work as a photographer is skillfully chronicled in her 2006 book entitled, Steve McQueen, the Last Mile.)

Even though Minty was actively involved in her modeling career, Steve asked the twenty-five-year old to move to California with him.

Tom Horn was to be Steve's last western movie, even though the actor had planned on making more films. The prospect of not having to go overseas for his next film appealed to the Hollywood veteran. Many critics claimed that the film strayed from the historical account of Horn's life, and by the mid '70s, the famous movie Star Wars had become the new western.

Steve McQueen had always had an on-going love affair and passion for his hobbies and toys whether it was a Ferrari sports car, an Indian motorcycle, a vintage Hudson Hornet vehicle or an old airplane. His fascination with vintage airplanes compelled him to purchase a 1940 Stearman biplane. The Stearman was a popular trainer for Navy pilots during World War II. Steve had mastered race car driving, dirt (motorcycle) biking and now a whole new world to conquer lay ahead of him—flying biplanes.

With a noticeably less demanding film schedule before him, Steve removed himself even further from the business that had taken him to fame. He realized his need to get out of the rat race and tried to associate with fewer celebrities and spend more time with "average" people. He found that he experienced the greatest peace when he escaped to isolated locations far away from the busy world of Hollywood. Steve found his place in the rolling hills of Santa Paula, located approximately sixty-four miles from Los Angeles. This community was much different from Hollywood, Beverly Hills or Malibu where a number of his peers lived. McQueen lived at his airplane hangar at Santa Paula for a few months, but in time he and Barbara found fifteen-acres with a 1896 ranch house which they called home.

The more passionate Steve became about flying, the more he needed an instructor who could teach him everything about flying vintage airplanes. Sammy Mason came highly recommended as an excellent instructor by folks around Santa Paula. Mason had the skill and experience that Steve was looking for.

Steve recognized, early on, that the elder Mason was a deeply religious man. Steve's relationship with Sammy, and Mason's son, Pete, progressed to a point where Steve sometimes talked to the Masons about God. In the book, Steve McQueen – the Last Mile, Barbara said that Steve once told Sammy, "There's something different about you ... but I can't quite put my finger on it." Mason replied, "That's because I'm a Christian, Steve." [78] Questions about God intrigued the actor enough to discuss these issues with people whom he felt he could trust.

Steve's martial arts instructor and friend, Pat Johnson, had also talked to Steve about God during the time when Steve got divorced, two years earlier. Because of their long friendship, Steve had confidence in his friend's advice and admired that kind of faith.

The seeds had been planted over the course of his lifetime. Now they were finally taking root, and once Steve decided to commit his life to Christ and become a Christian, the effect of his decision became clear to those around him. According to Barbara, Steve's "conversion to Christianity took place over the course of several years. With his natural paranoia, Steve never jumped into anything until he was absolutely sure there was no 'con' involved." [79] Steve's friend Grady Ragsdale, Jr. said, "I saw a dramatic change in Steve ... Oh, he still had the problems with his quick temper and with areas of his life that had been poorly cultivated for many years, but I doubt that I have ever seen a man flourish with more spiritual reality in such a short time." [80]

It was a fresh start for the actor. He enjoyed going to church with Barbara and his friends from the airport. As Barbara later noted in her book, "being born again in Christ was important to Steve, and helped him find the inner peace that had eluded him so long." Over a period of time, the two both enjoyed attending the Ventura Missionary Church.

Steve's last movie was The Hunter, a story of a modern day bounty hunter, Ralph 'Papa' Thorson. Steve was cast in the lead character's role. Kathryn Harrold played Thorson's love interest, Dotty. Ben Johnson, who was with Steve in The Getaway, played the part of Sheriff Strong. The final scene of the movie was touching. Steve (playing Thorson) affectionately holds his new born for the first time. The expression of Steve's face in the closing scene is priceless. [81]

During the filming of the Hunter, Steve began coughing more than normal. On the advice of a few friends, he decided to visit a doctor in Los Angeles. According to Entertainment Weekly, it was shortly after the filming of The Hunter that Steve received a diagnosis of lung cancer often related to exposure from asbestos. Naturally, the news hit him very hard and his family and friends were devastated. Steve was determined to not only beat the disease, but keep the news away from the media. Accomplishing both of these goals became difficult.

In an effort to show Barbara how much he really loved her, on January 16, 1980, the couple married at their ranch home in Santa Paula, California. His good friend, Sammy Mason, and his wife, Wanda, served as witnesses. The ten minute ceremony conducted by Leslie Miller from the Ventura Missionary Church was bittersweet. The couple had grown to know and love Miller during their weekly Bible study sessions.

Steve McQueen had always been a fighter, a competitor. He had proven this time and time again and overcame many obstacles throughout his long and illustrious career. When his doctor told him that his condition was inoperable, Steve wanted to pursue alternative types of cancer treatment. Steve and Barbara decided to meet with Dr. William Kelly of the International Health Institute (IHI). After meeting with Kelly at his ranch, Steve decided to use his services and begin treatment immediately.

Over the course of the ensuring months, Steve adhered to Kelly's advice and treatments which included "an arduous, three month regimen involving coffee enemas, animal cell injections, laetrile, and more than 100 vitamin and mineral pills a day...."[82] McQueen was convinced that the treatments from the Health Institute would improve his condition. His conversation with Grady Ragsdale, Jr. that October convinced his friend that he still had confidence in the treatment's success.

Billy Graham called McQueen on November 7, 1980, after getting word that Steve wanted to meet with him. Grady picked Dr. Graham up at his hotel room in Los Angeles and drove him to Steve's home in Santa Paula. In his personal remark's quoted in Grady Ragsdale's book, Rev. Graham recalls meeting with Steve that day. "Though I never met him before, I recognized him immediately from his pictures, even though he had lost considerable weight. His eyes were bright and shiny. He sat up in the bed and greeted me warmly. He told me of his spiritual experience. He said that about three months before he knew he was ill, he had accepted Christ as Savior and had started going to church, reading his Bible, and praying. He said he had undergone a total transformation of his thinking and his life ...."[83]

Dr. Graham fondly remembers spending several hours with Steve by praying and reading a number of passages of scripture with him. As Billy departed, he gave Steve his Bible and inscribed it to him. [84]

Continuing in his treatments, Steve travelled to El Paso, Texas and from there to a clinic in Juarez, Mexico. Surgery had been scheduled to remove a tumor in his stomach. Members of his family also travelled there for support. Grady last remembers seeing Steve clinging tightly to the Bible Dr. Graham had given him.

It was initially thought that the operation was a success. However, early the next morning the medical staff discovered that Steve had developed a blood clot which caused his heart to fail.

A number of days later at the Santa Paula ranch, Steve's family members (including Barbara, Ali, Neile, Chad, and Terry) and other close friends attended a memorial for the former actor. The memorial was conducted by Pastor Leonard DeWitt from the Ventura Missionary Church. He read from the 23rd Psalm ending with this verse: "Surely goodness and mercy shall follow me all the days of my life; and I shall dwell in the house of the Lord for ever" (RSV).

According to the Ventura County Star newspaper, Steve's friends from the Santa Paula airport flew a missing man formation over the memorial service with a blank space where McQueen would have been. [85]

Steve's legacy continues to this day, but it was his commitment to his God and enduring faith in his Savior that eternally altered the course of his life. Some say that Steve's journey ended the day of his death on November 7, 1980 but in reality, it had only just begun.

Chapter 4

Ruben "Lefty" De La Torre A Former Gang Leader's Remarkable Story

C hildren can be cruel and Rueben Torres knows firsthand how much truth lies behind that statement. Most children survive the physical teasing and taunting, but what happens to their tender hearts?

Attendants at San Diego's Mercy Hospital heard the cries of yet another baby boy, the child named Rueben De La Torre who entered the world on November 29, 1965. Looking at the welcomed infant, they had no clue who he would become. His parents lived in south San Diego, and later moved to the California community of San Ysidro, which straddles the US/Mexico border.

Rueben's father, a contractor and part-time chauffeur and his mother met in Tijuana, Mexico. They married in 1961 and between December '64 and April '67, brought four children into the world. Ruben was the second youngest of the four. All four roomed together in bunk beds in their San Ysidro home with Reuben always on a bottom bunk.

At the tender age of seven, Ruben realized that there was something seriously wrong with his hand and arm. At school, kids would tease him calling him crippled. Teasing from his peers seemed to follow him wherever he went.

Finally, the young boy decided to confront his parents and asked them what was wrong with his body. Ruben vividly remembers seeing his parents cry. He could not understand though, why no one hugged him. That night he retired to his room and scanned his body. For the first time, he clearly saw his crippled condition. His parents tried to protect their son but he continued to be a target for bullying.

Ruben hated his disfigurement, his body, and his life. He remembers telling his parents, "I am going to make you suffer ... I'm going to make the world suffer." That day, Ruben stopped loving himself. He stopped loving people and he started hating God.[86]

By the age of seven, Rueben continued to be plagued by malicious teasing from his class mates. They tormented him over something he had no control over. Kids teased De La Torre unmercifully and cruelly called him names.[87]

Ruben acted as if everything was all right, but it wasn't. Years later Ruben confessed that he hated school, but he had to pretend that he liked it.[88] No one really understood how beaten down and discouraged the young boy was. No one understood the anger that was growing inside him. He hated himself and he hated the world.

The Dangers of Gang Life

Because of his unmet needs, the rejected nine-year-old joined San Ysidro's local gang, Little Locos, just to fit in somewhere. Even though Ruben still lived at home, he became a stranger to his immediate family. His mother was distraught, but Ruben just didn't care. He'd found himself a new family—his "homies."

During the first few years with the gang they started calling him Lefty. Rueben had told his homies that his crippled hand and leg came as the result of a .38 revolver gunshot wound. It became a badge of honor for him. By his tenth birthday, he had already started experimenting with drugs and alcohol. His homies were older than Ruben but no one seemed to care. They taught Ruben what he needed to know about surviving on the street and his entire personality changed. He craved violence and enjoyed the wild side of his new lifestyle. In a never-ending quest for acceptance and respect, Reuben wanted to be feared. He soon became an angry person who was looking for death.[89]

About a year later Ruben was arrested for 'gang association' by local police authorities. When De La Torre failed to appear in court, the judge issued a bench warrant for his arrest. Ruben wound up in the county's juvenile facility. That arrest was the start of his lengthy rap sheet as well as the beginning of his life of crime.

Ruben's parents anguished over their son's involvement with the gang. They were also upset about his propensity for skipping school to hang out with his gang. Ruben received new charges of public drunkenness and being under the influence of an illegal substance. De La Torre became the guy who his friends looked up to. He recruited others into the gang and became invincible—or so he thought. Many years later, he shared how he never thought about the future. He continued to live a violent life; blood and death fascinated this teenager.

Gang growth was becoming a severe problem for law enforcement not only in Lefty's region of South Bay (around San Ysidro) but for the police throughout Southern California in the '80s. Ruben's troubles with the local authorities continued to get worse and the local police had become well acquainted with Lefty and his gang associations. The fifteen-year-old teenager became known as a gang veteran. A his rap sheet grew at an alarming rate, Lefty routinely found himself serving time in a number of local juvenile detention centers. Because of his age (and juvenile delinquency law), he never experienced incarceration with adults. At sixteen, Lefty found himself arrested for petty theft, possession of a deadly weapon (on school grounds) and a repeat conviction of his gang-activity indictment.

As the teenager's behavior continued to deteriorate, Lefty knew that someday he'd be serving time in state prison. Even so, the thought of such a penalty didn't slow him down for a second. He simply didn't care. His loyalty had now been pledged to a large gang called Sidro.

Lefty's troubles with the law followed him throughout his high school years. In his first two weeks as an 11th grader, he was jumped while on high school grounds. Ruben's retaliation for the assault resulted in expulsion. The teenager's continual brushes with the law caused him to be removed from three different high schools over a period of over two years. In an attempt to keep an earlier promise made to his mother (to obtain his high school diploma), Ruben eventually enrolled in the Montgomery / Mar Vista adult school in South San Diego.

The young man's dedication to his gang continued to grow. In his strange way of thinking, he believed that his homies fulfilled his personal need of acceptance. As he would say years later, "This fact alone didn't make me think about the consequences of my actions." [90] Nonetheless, it remained important for Ruben to fulfill the promise he once made to his mother and graduate from school. Even though he intensely disliked going to school, De La Torre tried to make good on his promise.

Ruben De La Torre finally stood in line to receive his high school diploma during the school's annual graduation ceremony in 1984. It was a proud moment for his mother and the teenager, even for someone so dedicated to the destructive lifestyle of gangs and crime. When called to the podium during that peaceful June afternoon, De La Torre walked to the stage, accepted his diploma and even shook hands with school officials.

Temptation overtook him. As Ruben strolled past the school's microphone, suddenly, he stopped. As he looked out over the audience, Ruben began to lift his fist high in defiance, and started shouting the name of his gang through the school's PA system.

According to the police, all hell broke loose! Everywhere around the auditorium fights broke out between rival gang members. Shots were fired and complete pandemonium ensued. As fists and knives were flailing, school administrators stood horrified. Sadly, one of Lefty's closest friends died in a bullet exchange. As the blood-drenched body of his friend lay on the concrete, Ruben remembers asking himself, "Why didn't it happen to me? Why wasn't I the one who was killed?" [91]

Off to Prison

Despite his attempt to escape local authorities, it took the police less than a day to find Ruben. The eighteen-year-old gang member was charged with attempted murder. Within several months Reuben received a sentence for one year in prison for the gang fight, and another three years for crashing into a police car during an attempted escape.[92] Ruben De La Torre, no longer a minor, had to face life as an adult felon.

He found the subculture in prison not much different than street life. Most of the prison population was socially divided by racial and ethnic categories. It didn't matter if you did time at Donovan, Chino Otay Lake or Soledad state prisons, there was a similarity in the culture within the prison walls. Gang members were always at odds with each other fights were common in prison. Revenge and retaliation within the prison population became an ever-present concern for the prisoners, their guards and wardens. Once Lefty had served his time he headed back to San Ysidro, to the same old friends and the same old lifestyle. Ruben confessed, "It was the only world I knew. It was the only life I felt secure in."[93]

He had not changed and it didn't take long before De La Torre found himself arrested again due to parole violations dealing with possession of heroin and methamphetamines. Once again, Ruben went back to prison. Upon his next release, he decided he'd try something different and took residence in a trailer park in Chula Vista, California. He supported himself with social security benefits for his disability and a part-time job. Eventually Ruben got fired from his job because of his excessive absences. He was addicted to the immediate gratification he found in robbing people. The police presented him again with new charges. This pattern of crime and punishment continued to plague De La Torre's and sadly, his response was not a positive one.

Getting an Education but Still a Criminal

Lefty walked out of the jail but this time he decided to enroll in a vocational school at UCI (United Education Institute). It had been sixteen years since his arrest for the adult school medley, and Reuben admitted, "I was tired of living the way I was living." Still, bad habits followed him as he continued to make poor choices. Ruben continued using illegal drugs but managed to graduate from vocational school that year and obtained a sales job marketing internet services.

Even upon earning his degree from vocational school, Ruben still couldn't break out of his long cycle of crime. Ruben appeared destined to continue this downward spiral and repeat his horrible habits for the rest of his life. This time police arrested Lefty for new crimes he'd never faced before—identity and credit card theft. With this De La Torre now faced the distinct possibly of serving life behind bars. Prosecutors convicted him on grand theft charges–a white collar crime.

In February of 2002 Rueben began serving his new felony conviction. At some point as he peered out of his cell, De La Torre realized that next time he would never be released again. With the enactment of California's new three strikes law, criminals faced stronger sentencing for repeat felonies. Ruben already had two strikes against him. A third strike on his adult criminal record would mean the end.

The aging Ruben realized that twenty years of his life had been wasted going in and out of prison. He finally understood the futility of his life of crime and how he had lost so many opportunities. At the age of forty, he felt that his dream of having children and raising a family someday were gone, forever.

He was an emotional wreck. While in prison Ruben heard from an old love interest who informed Ruben that he was the father of one of her kids. At first, De La Torre really didn't know what to say. Later, he was angry when he learned that she had lied to him. As Ruben put it, "She played with my manhood!"[94] Ruben became so enraged and obsessed with getting revenge that he decided to murder the woman upon his release. Even knowing that he faced the possibility of life in prison if he murdered this woman, hate consumed him.

Encountering Christ

De La Torre still had six months left on his sentence when his new cell mate moved in with him. His name was Raul, or "Pisa" as Ruben used to call him. Raul annoyed Ruben with his nightly prayer ritual, bible reading and church attendance. Lefty became so irritated with Raul that he took his cell mate's Bible and threw it away.[95]

Despite Ruben's opposition to his cellmate, Raul still tried to be his friend but the veteran gang member would have none of it. Regardless of what Ruben said or did, Raul wouldn't give up. Raul continued to tell Ruben how Jesus Christ had dramatically changed his life.

Raul was released from prison in June, which left Ruben alone in his cell.

Several weeks later, on June 28, 2006, Rueben Lefty De La Torre was finally released from prison. While he knew he wouldn't be given another chance for parole or pardon, he felt determined to kill the woman who had lied to him and betrayed him. Ruben was angry and wanted revenge!

Lefty contemplated connecting with old gang buddies. When he left the Mt. Carmel State Prison facility in Chino, California he had $200 in his pocket, a few scraps of paper and nowhere to go. With his limited resources, he searched through some old phone numbers for places to stay.

When he arrived back in San Diego, it was around 6:00 p.m. His situation didn't give him much choice – not at that hour; not without a car or any form of transportation. He dug around in his pocket and looked at the scraps of paper. On one, he found the name and number of a Henry Guzman, a person he'd never met before. Looking back, Lefty couldn't remember who gave him Guzman's name or number. He had to make a decision; stay on the street, reconnect with old homies or call this unknown number written on a crinkled, dirty piece of paper. The clock kept ticking and his stress was building. He called Guzman.

With an inability to trust anyone, Ruben moved out of his comfort zone. He stayed at the home of Henry Guzman that night. Henry and his family accepted the former felon into their home unconditionally. After a few weeks at the Guzman's San Ysidro home, some of Lefty's old barriers and walls of mistrust started to crumble.

De La Torre was especially touched by the way Henry treated him. Although difficult for him to believe that someone he hardly knew could trust him so much, he enjoyed his new environment. Henry told Ruben, "It was time for you to be given a chance because I believe in you." The trust that Henry provided to his guest touched Ruben down to the very core of his being.

Henry Guzman became a role model to the former convict. As the Director of Home Victory Outreach, Henry Guzman believed that the best way to touch the life of someone was to show them God's love. Henry knew that the Scriptures addressed this topic extensively. The Bible explains that one of the best ways to reach a person with such a troubled past is with love. "Love is patient, love is kind. It does not envy, it does not boast, it is not proud. It is not rude, it is not self-seeking, it is not easily angered, it keeps no record of wrong. Love does not delight in evil but rejoices in the truth. It always protects, always trusts, always hopes, always perseveres. Love never fails." [96]

Rueben Lefty Torres stepped into a church for the first time in decades on July 30, 2006. The man who just two months earlier had wanted to kill someone surrendered his life to Jesus Christ. It was a dramatic and life-changing moment for the forty-one year old man.

In December, Rueben began a new job as caretaker for the church's facility in San Ysidro. Over the next few years, the local church leadership gradually gave Ruben more responsibilities. The confidence they extended to De La Torre helped him start a new life.

The remarkable transformation continued in the life of this new disciple. As Ruben started opening up the pages of his Bible, he learned how to pray and counsel others. His own experiences gave him credibility that encouraged others. He even worked as a greeter for the San Ysidro church. Guzman suggested that he reach out to other men who were still involved with gangs in the area, and although the assignment was tough, he knew that Ruben had the potential to impact many lives.

God remarkably renewed a heart and life that government agencies, the California State Prison system, Reform schools, parole boards and government counseling services had pretty much given up on. Stories such as Ruben's demonstrate the incredible power of a God who lives and breathes through those who diligently dedicate themselves to Him.

Reaching out to gang members and Making a Difference!

Today Ruben De La Torre in San Ysidro assists men and women who have been imprisoned in the gang culture. The church, along with Victory Outreach's more than 500 other ministries worldwide, operates a home for formerly wayward gang members and street people. Church members work in these homes to help rehabilitate men from their former lifestyles. Victory Outreach operates homes for women as well. Members of Ruben's church have tirelessly and diligently tried to follow the Christian principles of love and charity that encourage men and women to leave their destructive lifestyles.

Over the years, there have been many dramatic examples of Victory Outreaches' impact in communities around the world (www. VictoryOutreach.org). In the '90s their San Diego church sponsored a play that portrayed the stark reality of gang life. Held in a large, historic auditorium in downtown San Diego, church congregants (some of whom were formerly involved in the gangs themselves) invited members of fourteen local gangs to attend the event. Not surprisingly, police authorities were convinced that there would be a rumble that night. As police officers took positions around the building, they found that their fears never materialized. At the play's conclusion that evening, Rev. Tony Guzman (Henry's brother) stepped forward and gave an altar call resulting in over 200 gang members turning in their weapons and committing their lives to Christ.

Today, Victory Outreach has ministries in thirty countries including most major population centers in Europe and North and South America. This worldwide ministry prides itself in being able to reach out to communities and neighborhoods that are plagued with drugs and gang violence. Their ministries have won recognition, awards and resolution proclamations from such diverse locations as Ireland, Holland, Scotland, India, the halls of Congress, California's State legislature, Atlanta, San Jose, and Los Angeles.

Victory Outreach's message of hope is grounded in the good news of the risen Savior, Jesus Christ. The ministry can point to the real lives of men and women like David and Eleanor Garcia, Henry Guzman, Ruben De La Torre and others who have not only seen the change in their own lives but in thousands of others who have been touched by the power of Jesus Christ. The ministry seeks to "inspire and instill within people the desire to fulfill their potential in life with a sense of dignity, belonging and destiny." [97]

Ruben Lefty De La Torre is a true testimony to the miracle-working power of God. Today, the former gang member works to restore the lives of men who are struggling with drugs and still living in the violent world of gangs. De La Torre faithfully serves in the 'court ministry' for the church. It's a ministry that works with local district attorneys in an effort to voluntarily place men and women with troubled pasts into homes run by Ruben's church. Unlike his violent past, Ruben now knows where to find peace, hope and joy. He also knows that while man may reject you, God never does! He has found his destiny in an eternal relationship with his Lord and Savior, Jesus Christ, who is always been there for him.

Chapter 5

Ronald Wilson Reagan Appointment with Destiny

R onald Wilson Reagan will probably be remembered in history
as one of the greatest Presidents of our time. British Prime
Minister Margaret Thatcher once said of our 40th President, "He
won the Cold War without firing a shot." From winning the Cold
War and overcoming communism, to dealing with inflation at home,
Reagan imparted hope with his unfailing optimism in the strength
of the American spirit.

February 6, 1911 was a great day for America! On that day the
future President was born. He was the second of two sons born to
John Edward and Nelle Clyde Wilson Reagan. The family lived in an
apartment on the second floor of a commercial building in Tampico,
Illinois. Neil, Ron's older brother, was born several years earlier
in 1908.[98]

Ron's father, John, (aka Jack) by his friends, considered himself
a merchant by trade and had no strong religious convictions. Nelle,
his mother, was a homemaker with Scotch, Irish and English heritage
who showed great devotion to her Protestant Christian faith.

Due to his father's lack of employment, life presented a challenge
for the Reagan family during young Ronald's formative years. They
moved frequently, living in a variety of communities in northern
Illinois, but eventually settled down in Dixon, IL. Reagan's mother
dedication to her faith drew her to a local Disciples of Christ Church

close enough to where she and her two young sons could regularly attend the church's weekly services.[99]

One blustery winter night young Ron found his father intoxicated and sprawled out in the snow in front of their home. The eleven-year-old boy had to drag his father back inside. Seeing his father's condition not only disappointed Reagan, but it also impacted his future outlook on life. The incident helped draw young Ron closer to the Christian faith of his mother.

Nelle's dedication to her faith was demonstrated by the many hours she freely gave in volunteer service to the church. Besides leading the church's regular prayer meetings, Nelle also routinely visited the local prison and convalescent homes telling them about the good news of Jesus Christ. Ron's mother remained a positive influence in her son's youth. Years later, Reagan recalled the powerful influence his mother had on his life by saying that "my mother always told me that God has a plan for my life."

Ronald loved to read. He took an interest in reading a book titled *That Painter of Udell* by Harold Bell Wright. The book had a profound effect on the young Reagan. He identified with the book's leading character, Dick Falkner, who grew up in poverty with an alcoholic father. The Painter, written in 1903, taught Ron that being a Christian involved more than going to church once a week. It focused on following Christ, developing a strong character and becoming a true disciple. Ronald realized that Falkner lived his life much as his mother was doing. Not long afterward, Reagan decided he wanted to be baptized at his mother's church and make a public profession of his faith.[100]

While conscious of his father's struggles with alcohol, he still retained a keen admiration and respect for his commitment to supporting his family. Ronald knew his family was struggling with finances but things started to look up when his father accepted employment managing a small shoe store in Dixon.

Ron, nicknamed Dutch by his father, became actively involved in the First Christian Church of Dixon. He taught Sunday school, participated in church plays and was influenced by his association with the church's pastor, Ben Cleaver. Years later Reagan shared with the minister in a letter stating that he "was grateful ... for a faith in which you played a part in instilling within me." Cleaver served as a father figure during the time when young Ron needed guidance the most. [101]

Reagan was on the Dixon High School football team, and accepted roles in several plays at his school. During the summer, the teenager worked as a lifeguard at nearby Lowell Park where he developed a reputation as an exceptional lifeguard by saving dozens of lives. [102]

The Lowell Park job enabled Reagan to stash away money for school. Ronald hoped that his athletic ability on the football field combined with his outside work would enable him to afford college. He won a scholarship to play college football at Eureka College (in Eureka, Illinois). Founded in 1855, the college was associated with the Disciples of Christ denomination and also had a performing arts department with an excellent reputation. It was there that Reagan participated in sports, student government and joined the (TKE) fraternity. He gave their senior class commencement address; for the first time in June of 1957 and again in May of 1982 and each time emphasized that "everything good that happened to me started here (at Eureka)." [103] Clearly, Reagan's years at the college were endearing to him.

Reagan graduated from college and sought work as a radio announcer in the summer of 1932. He wanted to become a radio announcer and after interviewing with the NBC radio affiliate in Chicago, the radio network personnel suggested that he get first get some experience with a small, local station from an outlining community.

He followed their advice and eventually got his break. Reagan was hired as a sports announcer for a small station (WOC) in Davenport, Iowa. By that next spring, one of his original contacts (at the station) left his job and the radio station hired Reagan to replace him. Living during the Great Depression, Reagan felt grateful to be earning $100 a month. Later, Ronald persuaded his station's management to have a seasoned announcer help him hone his craft and as he was a quick study, the experiment worked to Reagan's benefit. [104]

Less than two dozen radio stations gained noteworthy status during the 1930s. In Des Moines, Iowa, radio station WHO announced that it would consolidate its operation with its other sister station WOC.

As the parent company, radio station WHO now became Ronald's new employer.

Carrying one of the strongest radio signals in the Midwest, Reagan's station could reach more people over the air than the young broadcaster had conceived possible. The station had signed a contract to broadcast the Major League Chicago Cubs baseball games. Ron became the likely announcer to cover the games which forced him to become particularly adept at using expressive language and creative imagery in describing the statistics and occurrences of each of their games as they were relayed to him.

Doing the play-by-play announcing for the Cubs' games gave Ron, now in his mid '20s, quite a bit of regional prominence. Reagan's new found fame around the midwest afforded him outside opportunities as well. Ron earned money for appearances and speaking engagements and used that money to supplement his parent's income. It was economically devastating time for most Americans. The responsibility that he felt toward his parents was something he had learned as a boy and had been reinforced by his mother's Bible teachings.

For the next several years Dutch Reagan continued to do play-by-play radio announcing for the Cubs. During the 1937 baseball pre-season, Reagan accompanied the National League Chicago team to its exhibition games with their LA farm team, the Angels. After traveling many hours by train, the team finally checked into LA's Biltmore Hotel. That night Reagan happened to spot Joy Hodges, an old acquaintance, who used to work for WHO. Hodges was working as a singer with a local band performing at the Biltmore. As Reagan spoke to her that night, he mentioned his long time dream and aspiration of becoming an actor. Joy supplied him with the name of an agent she had once used. [105]

The very next day Reagan met with Bill Meiklejohn, a Hollywood talent agent. Meiklejohn was impressed with the young Reagan and requested a screen test from a casting director friend of his. Within a few days, and with a few pages of script in hand, Reagan had his screen test. Everything happened very quickly because his schedule with the Cubs required him to leave town within a few days. Knowing this, the casting director showed the film to his boss, studio executive

Jack Warner, who offered the aspiring actor a contract. [106] It was an amazing sequence of events, especially because it occurred during a time of unprecedented economic uncertainty.

Warner Brothers had quite a reputation in the movie making business during the era. Their studio was founded in 1923 by four brothers; Sam, Harry, Jack and Albert Warner. The rise of the Warner studio was clearly an American success story. The studio had put together a number of notable features during its early years whose casts included such well known actors as Humphrey Bogart, James Cagney, Edward G. Robinson, Joan Crawford, Gary Cooper, and Betty Davis.

Going to Hollywood

In June of 1937 Reagan left Des Moines and relocated to Los Angeles embarking on a whole new career. Reagan's first movie was Love Is in the Air. Typecast in what was considered a 'B' movie, Reagan looked at this experience as an opportunity to make his mark in this new profession. Reagan was determined to be the best movie actor he could be.

Between 1937 and 1943, Dutch had roles in thirty-one Warner films. One of Reagan's better known movies Knute Rockne – where he played an all American that seemed to be a perfect fit. This 1940s release was about Notre Dame's famous 1920s coach and football legend, Knute Rockne. In the film, the twenty-nine year old actor played the coach's star player, George Gipp. Rockne was played by actor Pat O'Brien. Reagan is still remembered for the famous line from the film, "Tell them to go out there with all they've got and just win one for the Gipper." The phrase, 'Win one for the Gipper' later became a rallying cry for Ronald Reagan and his followers through Reagan's years in politics. [107]

Reagan invited his parents to leave their midwest home and join him in Los Angeles. Ron purchased the first home they'd ever owned. It was close enough to his house that Ron could regularly visit them. His father Jack suffered from a weak heart and wasn't able to undertake any stressful jobs. His son hired him to answer his fan mail. [108]

Unfortunately, Jack's condition worsened, and he died on May 18, 1941. Although those days were difficult for Ron and his mom, Ron was convinced his father was in a better place and finally at peace with God. His mother provided the strong emotional and spiritual support needed to help her son through his grief. Years later Reagan recalled how his mother reminded him of the knowledge of the happiness and solace to be gained by talking to the Lord during a special ceremony celebrating the National Day of Prayer (in 1986).[109]

Reagan continued to act in a variety of Warner Brother's movies. One film, Brother Rat, depicted student life at the Virginia Military Institute. Reagan became close friends with one of the film's co-stars, Jane Wyman. It did not take long for that romance to blossom, and in 1940; Ronald Reagan and Jane Wyman were married. For the next five years, the couple lived in Hollywood where they had one biological daughter, Maureen Elizabeth Reagan (1941). Several years later the couple adopted a son, Michael E. Reagan. The young family attended the Beverly Hills Christian Church. Ron's mother took an active role in the family and still continued to visit prisons and even did some volunteer work for a local sanitarium.

Another world war was looming on the horizon. Reagan later remembered receiving a letter three months after Pearl Harbor (12/07/1941) from the War Department. Even before he slipped his finger between the seal, he already knew what it said. Written on the outside portion of the letter were the words: immediate action.

The harsh realities of World War II affected everyone during those tumultuous times. Ron received a combat deferment because of his poor eyesight; however, the military made good use of his skills. The thirty-one-year-old actor became a member of the military's motion picture unit; responsible for training and producing educational films for the Army. The war's end in 1945 was enthusiastically embraced by everyone.

Reagan soon became active again in the Hollywood circles, and by 1946 he began rubbing elbows with members of the Screen Actors Guild. They were impressed with Reagan and he became president of the group during a time when Americans' concerns about communism had reached an all-time high. Much to the consternation of some of his Hollywood peers, Ron took a strong stand against this form of tyranny. He expressed his concern over communist sympathizers, warning of the dangers of atheistic communism.

Like his father Jack, Ronald had long considered himself an FDR Democrat and even memorized President Roosevelt's 1933 inaugural address. However during the late '40s Reagan felt his maturing political philosophy lined up more with Dwight D. Eisenhower. Eisenhower was the commander of the WWII forces during the invasion of Normandy. In the late '40s Reagan's belief system was more aligned with his mother's conservative, Christian upbringing.

Reagan also realized he had lost some luster as a Hollywood star by the time the war ended. Gone were the marquee roles that had been his in the pre-war days. Up until then, Reagan considered his best acting performance to have taken place seven years earlier in King's Row. The film, released by Warner Brothers studios in 1942, starred Ann Sheridan, Robert Cummings and Ronald Reagan.

Reagan's wife, Jane Wyman, had continued her own successful career in films. Her 1948 role in Johnny Belinda earned her an academy award for best actress, however during that same period Wyman sought a divorce from her husband of eight years.

News of the divorce devastated the thirty-seven-year old actor. He felt the pain of failure. He became convinced that Wyman was "sick and nervous and not herself." [110] Reagan was dedicated to his family, and couldn't imagine giving up. Knowing of her youngest son's plight, Nelle spent time praying for Ron and his family. God answered his mother's prayers.

The melancholy of the four year period since his breakup with Wyman finally ended. Nancy Davis, an up and coming actress whom Reagan had met through the Screen Actors Guild, became his ray of sunshine. Their March 4, 1952 marriage ceremony was witnessed by friends William Holden and Brenda Marshall, among others. Later that year Ron and Nancy Reagan welcomed into their family their new daughter, Patti. Around six years later son, Ron Jr., was born in May of 1958.

Unlike a number of actors in Hollywood during the early 1950s, Reagan did not view television entertainment as an inferior medium for people in his profession. Television in the early 50's was a new media and relatively expensive for most Americans. The free broadcasts were mostly limited to watching only major networks in larger communities. Reagan saw the potential of this new form of entertainment and he also needed a job. He found it with the General Electric (GE) Theater.[111]

The General Electric Theater made its debut in July of 1953 on prime time television. The Theater offered a weekly thirty minute drama production with some pretty well known Hollywood stars including Natalie Wood, Jimmy Stewart, Cary Grant, Walter Matthau, Michael Landon, and Joan Crawford. In September of 1954 the show's sponsor, the General Electric Company, added its one and only host—Ronald Reagan.

Becoming a Conservative Spokesman and Politician

It was a great move not only for Ronald Reagan but also for GE. Within a few months, the Reagan hosted program rose in the Nielsen ratings achieving a place in the top ten ratings status. What a remarkable achievement! The introduction of Reagan, as the weekly TV drama's host, had been a wise choice.

The success of the program helped Reagan gain exposure across the country. During his tenure as host, (1954-1962), Reagan made more than 130 appearances at various GE plants around the county as a public relations representative. Reagan's television notoriety became a launching pad for things to come. Throughout this entire period, Reagan continued to believe that God had a plan for his life and it certainly seemed to be playing out – even during his early days in television in the 1950s.

General Electric decided to discontinue its highly successful program due to a controversy between GE and Reagan that involved Reagan's public warning about the dangers of big government. Reagan found his political voice and became active as he toured the country as a conservative spokesman.

Reagan made the decision to jump into politics during the 1964 Presidential election. As Reagan often noted, "I didn't leave the Democrat party, the party left me." [112] The actor's philosophical support for Republican Senator Barry Goldwater persuaded him to get involved in his friend's campaign for President. During the '64 Presidential campaign Reagan gave his famous "A Time for Choosing" speech. This highly publicized and televised speech delivered in the fall of 1964 convinced friends and influential California Republicans to encourage Reagan to run for Governor. [113]

After his success as host for GE Theater, Reagan had signed on to be the host of the syndicated television show, Death Valley Days, which had a long run on TV dating back to 1952. Ron's tenure as host was cut short by his entrance into politics.

At the age of fifty-four, the former President of the Screen Actors Guild declared his candidacy for Governor of California in January of 1966 as the Republican nominee. He faced off with Democrat incumbent Governor Pat Brown. Californians had a clear choice for Governor: liberal incumbent Brown or the conservative challenger, Reagan. The Republican candidate's support from California's business community was overwhelming. That fall (1966) the Republican candidate ran on his long held beliefs of small government and his advocacy of representing the California taxpayer. Brown quickly attacked Reagan's lack of experience. The Democrat Governor even brought in Senator Edward 'Ted' Kennedy from Massachusetts to campaign against Reagan. As Election Day approached, Brown's personal attacks continued. The Democrat Governor ran a television commercial that showed him standing before a group of children saying, "I'm running against an actor, and you know who killed Abe Lincoln, don't you?" That November, Reagan was elected by a whopping 58% to a 42% margin. As a fiscal conservative, it didn't take long for the new Governor to learn what lay ahead of him. Reagan later admitted, "I was about to stick my head into the lions' den and the lions would be waiting for me". On January 2, 1967, Ronald Reagan was sworn into office by California Justice Marshall F. McCombs. [114]

Reagan became Governor during a fairly turbulent time in California's history. Many of the high profile California State and public universities were experiencing problems. Unrest at the state's colleges was caused by student's consternation over America's participation in the war in Vietnam in the early 1960's. Also, in 1967 the California State Assembly was controlled by a hostile Democrat legislature. Reagan's election as governor did not by any means convince the legislature that his philosophy of small and efficient government was right for the golden state.

Reagan acknowledged in his memoirs that upon taking office in 1967, he was surprised by the level of budgetary problems that actually existed in the state government. The new governor approached the problem like any good business executive. Reagan and his administration team decided to hire the best business minds they could find. It was their assignment to locate the financial inefficiencies of more than fifty state agencies. The commission remained dedicated to identifying areas where the budget could be cut, as California was facing deep financial trouble. Reagan reluctantly made a decision that he did not want to do; he raised taxes. [115]

The strain of office took its toll on the new Governor. Now in his mid fifties Ronald developed a stomach ulcer. He recalled in his memoirs how two different men approached him saying that they were both part of prayer groups that regularly prayed for the California Governor. This deeply touched Reagan. When he next met with his doctor for his annual check-up, Reagan was pleasantly surprised to find the ulcer gone. Were the prayer groups a coincidence or a direct answer to prayer? It can be accurately said, "Just as millions of Americans believe in God, the former actor also believed in the power of prayer". [116]

Reagan decided to make the pledge that if the state had a budget surplus, he would refund taxpayers the difference. In 1968 he fulfilled that pledge. Reagan also made good use of the line item veto. It allowed him to cut some of the waste he saw in the legislative proposals. In fact, the line item veto became so effective that he used it over 900 times during his days as California governor. [117]

During the '60's and '70's the country experienced skyrocketing growth of government welfare programs and subsidies. It was also during the Johnson Administration (1963-1968) that the federal government initiated the so-called "war on poverty." This and similar subsidies quadrupled in California. The golden state had become the welfare state. California welfare claims represented 16% of all welfare payouts in the nation. Reagan became determined to tackle this issue. Coming from a poor background, Reagan clearly understood the need for charity. He realized the necessity of state welfare, but only for the truly needy. Philosophically, the Governor disagreed with the loose standards that state bureaucrats had previously set. He believed work for able bodied residents to be noble, honorable and necessary. Reagan had learned this during his early years with his mother Nelle and her strong Christian influence on him.

Reagan became convinced that just freely handing out public money was irresponsible and that excesses of the system needed to be brought under control. Both he and Democrat Speaker of the Assembly, Bob Moretti, eventually put together a plan that could be fair to the tax payers as well as reasonable and compassionate—especially for the truly needy. During Reagan's last two years in office, welfare rolls actually decreased for the first time in almost fifteen years. Through effective job training programs, thousands of former welfare recipients would help restore their own self dignity as they found jobs in the private sector. [118] Reagan felt particularly proud of the fact that his administration had delivered several year-end refunds to the taxpayers because of his state budget cuts.

Author and speechwriter, Paul Kengor, cited in a 2001 interview with William F. Clark, (Reagan's close friend and confidante) that Reagan prayed regularly during his eight years in office as Governor. The demands of his job caused stress and anxiety at times and Reagan strongly felt that prayer was needed for guidance.

Reagan's second term in office as California's governor expired in early 1975. The former California Governor, actor, and TV host was commissioned to get back into a medium where he had first become known to so many Americans. He went back to the radio. Over the course of next four years, Reagan produced hundreds of short radio commentaries. The broadcasts were heard on over 280 radio stations each week. His commentaries were also picked up by over 200 newspapers as well. The addresses gave the American public a unique glimpse into the personal and public beliefs of a man who was still only known to millions of Americans by his appearances on TV and the movie screen.

There appeared to be nothing that he would not discuss on radio and he proved it when he tackled religion in the public place. Clearly by his tone Reagan voiced disapproval of the 1963 Supreme Court removal of prayer from our public schools. In his April 17th commentary the former Governor addressed the Founding Fathers perspective of religion. "Having seen the domination of governments by a religious order or those nations where religious belief was dictated by government, the framers of our Constitution made sure that our nation's federal government would not favor a church and religion like what had been done in England (during the colonial times). They simply meant that individuals would be free to worship as they chose. Our federal government could not favor or discriminate against particular religions or denominations, nor could any denominations assume a role in government." [119]

Reagan felt some powerful emotions but with the encouragement of his friends and financial supporters, he decided to challenge incumbent President Gerald Ford for the Republican nomination for President that year. Could he pull it off? Did he have enough experience to sway the voters? When the Republican convention ended that year on August 18, 1976, the former California Governor had experienced a narrow loss (1187 to 1070 delegates) to the eventual nominee President Gerald R. Ford.

At the conclusion of the convention, Ron gave a short closing speech. The response to Reagan's speech was overwhelming. Former Pennsylvania Senator Richard Schwelker later described what happened by saying, "When the convention was over and we were all preparing to leave, we first had a gathering of the campaign workers at the hotel ballroom. There was hardly a dry eye in the house. Clair (my wife) went over to Governor Reagan and thanked him for all he had done and how he had conducted himself. (Ron) said, 'Well Claire, you shouldn't be upset about the outcome because it wasn't part of God's plan.'" [120]

Americans celebrated the 200th anniversary of our country's founding in 1976 with one event after another. During that year, the voters elected Georgia Governor Jimmy Carter as President. Many historians agree that Carter had a disappointing term in office. In his first year as President (in September of 1977) Carter agreed to give the Panama Canal back to Panama, causing much angst around the country. Also during Carter's last year in office the Iranian radical Islamic fundamentalists took over the American Embassy in Tehran and held fifty-two American hostages over 440 days. Many questioned Carter's inept handling of the economy. Carter's one and only term in office caused Americans to experience a severe period of stagflation as well as serious nationwide fuel shortages. It appeared that someone had stamped "weak" across the 39th President's forehead.

Truly America needed a change. Inflation took off (with interest rates in the 20% range) and many Americans were demoralized over the Iranian hostage crisis. Once again there was a ground swell of support for the sixty-nine year old former Governor. Ronald Reagan's optimistic rhetoric was infectious. Reagan decided to embark for one more run for the Presidency. He said, "If I could be elected President, I wanted to do what I could do to bring a spiritual revival in America. I believed that America's greatest years were ahead of it, that we had to look at the things that made it the greatest, richest, and most progressive country on the earth in the first place, decide what went wrong, and then put it back on course." [121]

In Reagan's 1980 campaign, a total of seven Republicans ran for the Presidential nomination. Up until the New Hampshire primary, Bush had been the most popular candidate, winning the Iowa primary just weeks prior but clearly a turning point occurred during the New England state's primary debate. Bush's advisors believed that only the top two candidates should appear in the televised debate. Reagan sided with the other candidates (Dole, Baker, Crane, Anderson, and Connally) who believed there should be more. When Reagan tried to explain the predicament, one news editor told the technical crew to turn off Reagan's microphone. Annoyed by the tactic, Reagan countered, "I paid for this microphone..." [122] and the audience went wild.

The California Governor went on to win the New Hampshire primary with over 51% the vote. Considering the number of candidates in the race, the results were amazing! While on the campaign trail that year, Adrian Rogers, the leader of the Southern Baptist Convention interviewed Reagan. Rogers directly asked the candidate, "Do you know the Lord Jesus Christ or do you simply know about Him?" Reagan responded declaring, "I know Him!" [123] Reagan's primary opponent, George Bush, joined the other five Republican opponents and resigned from the race by May of 1980. He had to wonder if this time would be different. Those gnawing questions again tried to creep in to derail his confidence and faith.

Senator Ted Kennedy challenged President Carter for the Democratic nomination that year. Carter won the Democratic Party nomination to face the Republican nominee, Ronald Reagan. By the fall, Carter and Reagan arranged a series of Presidential debates. Close friend and future Attorney General Ed Meese remembers one particular event when Reagan "asked for a few minutes of prayer" with some of his closest confidants prior to the nationally televised debate.[124] That November, Reagan won a sweeping victory over Carter. The Republican nominee won all but six states in the country. Reagan pulled off an amazing confirmation of his popularity. Now, more than ever, Ronald realized that he would need the wise counsel of the Holy Spirit to see him through the next few years.

Ronald Reagan placed his hand on his mother's old Bible and took the oath of office on January 21, 1981. He had not even set foot inside the oval office and yet the challenges set before him were already rapidly growing from his distracters as were their complaints, rumors, and lack of trust in his abilities. America was sinking into a recession with as severe an inflationary cycle as many people had seen in their lifetimes.

Reagan's initial challenges in office paled in contrast to the trial he faced March 30, 1981, when a crazed John Hinckley Jr. attempted to kill him. Hinckley's bullet came within an inch of piercing the President's heart. Looking back on that day, Reagan believed in God's divine intervention, protection and guidance even more. After being released from the hospital, Reagan wrote on his first night back at the White House that "whatever happens now, I owe my life to God and will try to serve Him every way I can." [125]

Years later Reagan wrote that as he prayed and asked for God's help while in the hospital, he felt the need to pray for "the mixed up young man that tried to assassinate him." Confessing this need, Reagan wrote that he began to pray for his soul. [126]

From that point on, Reagan and his wife Nancy grew reluctant to go to church (during his term on office) because of the possibility of putting church members in harm's way. Nevertheless, the President's long time advisor, Ed Meese, secretly left the White House on several occasions to pray with the President at St. John's Episcopal Church (which is located across from the White House and near LaFayette square). [127]

President Reagan had a reputation of surrounding himself with skilled and prudent advisors in his administrative White House team. Unlike his predecessor, Carter, who regularly got caught up in the details of his office, Reagan delegated tasks to able and knowledgeable staffers. The President had a gift of inspiring and encouraging the everyday citizen in our country during a time in the early '80s when strong leadership and direction were greatly needed.

Most Keynesian economists viewed the new President's fiscal plan of cutting federal taxes to revive the economy as foolish and risky. Nevertheless, it worked. By the end of 1983, the national economy started to rebound after more than three and a half years of sluggishness. Unlike his two terms as California Governor, Reagan did not have the luxury of the line item veto. His (Democrat) political opponents on the Hill wouldn't allow Reagan to make the spending cuts in government that they had promised. He learned that there were many unkempt promises in politics.

The 40th President "never wore his religion on his sleeve. Reagan remained private about his beliefs" but if "a private conversation (religion) came up, he could talk about the Bible with authority." [128] Reagan's beliefs enabled him to take a moral position on matters of social concern. His deep religious beliefs enabled the President and wife Nancy to take a stand against illegal drug abuse. Nancy Reagan committed herself to stopping drug abuse and lent her support to rehab programs as well as other forms of drug education.

President Reagan remained steadfast in building up and restoring the capability of the U.S. armed forces. Many of the Democrats during the Carter years did not share this view. "Recognizing the futility of the arms race and the hair trigger risk of annihilation it posed" [129] development of a strategic defense system (SDI) made sense. The President insisted that SDI would put untold financial pressure on the Soviet regime. Many agree today that the development of the defense system indirectly resulted in the demise of that government.

By 1984, Reagan became aware that he needed another four years in office to accomplish some of the goals he'd set in '81. In November 1984, the Reagan/Bush ticket won an overwhelming victory over the Democrat candidates Walter Mondale and Geraldine Ferraro. (Ferraro was the first woman to ever run as a VP candidate (from a major party) in our history). Reagan won almost 59% of the vote and won 49 of 50 states in the Electoral College vote. The Chief Executive embraced a stunning victory at the age of seventy-three. [130]

There were many remarkable events that occurred during Reagan's second term. Perhaps the most historically positive change resulting from Reagan's Presidency didn't occur until ten months after he left office. On November 9, 1989, East Germany allowed its citizens, (for the first time in more than forty years), to freely cross the border between East and West Germany.

During those key days of November, East Germans as well as many other Soviets were overwhelmed with joy! The menacing Berlin Wall tumbled down. Finally they could experience freedom. Just prior to his meeting with the President in 1988, Soviet Premier Gorbachev reopened hundreds of churches throughout Russia for the first time in decades.

In some way, shape or form, Reagan had always promoted liberty and freedom and now here there was religious freedom. Reagan shared some rather harsh and critical words with the Soviets for actively supporting atheism and tolerating religious persecution. Maybe his words had not fallen on deaf ears during the three previous meetings with Gorbachev. The change in policy in '88 signaled a breakthrough for that region's faith community. Eastern Europeans were finally free and Ronald Reagan as well as Pope John Paul II and Lech Walesa were key players in making it happen. [131]

Towards the end of his last year as President, Michael Reagan recounted a special moment on one Good Friday (in '88) when he joined his father on Air Force One for a trip from the East coast to Ventura County. Michael remembered seeing dad counting to nine on his fingers and his father proudly shared with his son, "In nine months, I'll be able to go to church again." [132]

It didn't take Ronald Reagan long to fulfill his wish. Even though he had his distracters in the media, the former President received numerous accolades from his admirers outside the beltway. To many Americans, Reagan was considered the greatest President to serve in the White House during their lifetime. His popularity remains unmatched by few Presidents in the last half century.

On June 5, 2004 Ronald Wilson Reagan left this world for the next. Memories of his illustrious professional career as a sports radio broadcaster, film actor, WWII veteran, television host, governor, and President were celebrated by millions of admirers on the day that he was finally put to rest as they sang the beautiful hymn Jerusalem. [133]

Regardless of his fame, achievements, notoriety or wealth, the scriptures tell us that ultimately God's primary interest is what did we do with our relationship with Jesus Christ. Thanks to God's enduring faithfulness, we can be sure that Ronald has already heard the words, "Well done, thy good and faithful servant."

Chapter 6

Oden Fong A Near Death Experience

T he Fong family had deep roots in the west, dating back to the discovery of gold in Sutter's Mill in 1848. The Gold Rush brought thousands of people to California in the 1850s including Oden Fong's great-grandfather. During the mid-eighteenth century, America's railroads were in the midst of a great expansion. Expansion of the rail roads enabled traveling Americans to move west to places such as California, Oregon, Washington and other western territories.

Oden's great-grand father, along with many other immigrants from China, moved to California, hoping to find steady work and a better life for themselves. Eventually he ended up settling in San Francisco. Oden's grandfather, Toon Fong, was born in the bay area but later moved to Sacramento, the state capital. After years of hard work and a little luck, Toon became one of the wealthier entrepreneurs in the region. According to his grandson, Toon owned a number of businesses, including a gambling operation (which was considered illegal in those days). [134]

Oden's father, Benson Fong, was born in 1916. Benson grew up with his three sisters in a relatively affluent environment when he was very young. That all changed with the coming of the Great Depression in 1929. The family fortune Benson's father worked so hard to acquire suddenly collapsed. Things became so bleak that his mother took Benson and his siblings and moved back to China.

Eventually young Benson decided to return to America. Benson moved to Maryville (near Sacramento) and worked at a local grocery store.

The Japanese attack on Pearl Harbor on the morning of December 7, 1941 signaled a period of change for everyone in America including the Fong family. Almost overnight the country was thrown into worldwide conflict after Japan's surprise attack on the U.S. naval fleet in Honolulu. America's involvement in a war in the Far East catapulted Hollywood studios into producing a series of war movies. Asian actors were needed to fill supporting character roles. Oden Fong's father life was about to take a dramatic turn.

Benson Fong had no formal training in acting, yet, when he heard from a local talent agent that Hollywood studios were looking for Asians to fill movie roles, he jumped at the opportunity. As Oden recalls, his father tested well. He won a supporting role in his first film. Fame came quickly to the actor when Benson played in the Charlie Chan movies in the '40s.

Some of the credits from over 50 movies that Benson Fong appeared in include: Thirty Seconds Over Tokyo (1944), Charlie Chan's the Chinese Cat (1944), Charlie Chan's the Red Dragon (1945), Dark Alibi (1946), Calcutta (1947), Peking Express (1951), His MajestyO'Keefe (1954), Conquest of Space (1955), Flower Drum Song (1961), Our Man Flint (1966), the Love Bug (1968), Kung Fu (1972) and Oliver's Story (1978). [135]

It was during Benson Fong's acting career that he met and married a young, talented actress by the name of Gloria Suie Chin, known as Maylia. Maylia had also found early success in her acting career.

Life in the 1950s and early '60s was good for the Fong household. With the prodding of his friend and actor Gregory Peck, Benson decided to open a restaurant on Hollywood's Sunset and Vine Street. The restaurant, Ah Fongs, was to become a favorite meeting place for local celebrities.

Oden Fong (the second oldest sibling in the family) was born in Hollywood, California on February 27, 1950. It wasn't long before the Fong family could afford to move into an upscale house on almost an acre of land in the Hollywood Hills. Gloria Fong assumed primarily responsibility for raising the young family as Benson worked long hours at the restaurant. Oden still has fond memories of his early childhood. Celebrities such as Burt Lancaster, Jack Lemon, Fred Astaire, Gregory Peck and June Allison were part of his young life. All were frequent guests at his father's restaurant. [136]

While many Chinese boys had a reputation for excelling in academics, Oden found himself drawn to creative endeavors such as music and art. Elvis Presley was one of Oden's earliest musical influences. Benson's good friend, Colonel Tom Parker was Elvis Presley's business manager and Oden received many autographed pictures and gifts from Presley. In 1962, Oden's father co-starred with Presley in his film Girls, Girls, Girls.

Despite his fortunate childhood, Oden's teenage years were not as pleasant. It was a white man's world, in a white era. Because of his ethnicity, Oden often got into fights defending himself from bullies who would poke fun at him for being Chinese. His days at Le Conte Junior High were marked with many bruises. [137]

Music became an escape for Oden, even starting at age ten. In grammar school he learned how to play the cello and guitar. Oden didn't learn to play the guitar by taking lessons; he learned to play from observing friends and reading books. By the time Oden turned twelve, he got his first electric guitar and soon entered local talent shows. His youngest sister, Lisa, remembered going to the Shrine Auditorium to see her brother play in a Battle of the Bands event. Surf music became popular and Oden added it to his ever-growing repertoire.

The fifteen year old student entered high school in 1965 and admitted that he only completed the bare minimum to get by. As a new student at Hollywood High, Oden decided to immerse himself in sports and music. His father nagged him and felt irritation that his son didn't bring home the good grades that he was capable of earning. Sports helped Oden cope with his father's disappointment. As a member of his high school's football team, Oden learned to enjoy the camaraderie of being a team member.

During his senior year in 1967, Oden began dating a girl whom he had known as a "friend" for years. She began experimenting with drugs and introduced Oden to them. As Oden later recalled in an interview, "my female friend (introduced) me to drugs ... turning me on to pot (and) LSD." [138] Within a relatively short period of time, Oden went from a clean-cut football player to a member of the counter-culture.

The eighteen year old started to spend a lot of time hanging out at various music establishments around west Los Angeles. Sunset Boulevard in west Hollywood near Beverly Hills and other spots close by became the hang-out address for a large number of young people. Famous entertainment establishments and night clubs such as the Whiskey-A-Go-Go, Gazarris, The Galaxy, The Troubadour, The Ash Grove and others attracted young customers who were drawn by the steady flow of rock music groups who regularly played at these local entertainment establishments.

Oden's father had hoped his son would have had a different life-style. The tension between them became so strained that after his graduation in June of 1968 Oden decided to move out. Everything about him changed. He let his hair grow long but would "tie his hair in a ponytail and tuck it into his shirt" out of respect for his father. [139]

The Hollywood High graduate and his girlfriend moved into a cheap apartment during the summer of 1968. He worked at a car wash, but quickly learned that selling drugs provided a more lucrative income. Oden came to believe that drugs altered how he felt about people and they somehow raised him above the sheltered world of his childhood into the 'real world'. Deceived into thinking that his drug use made him more cerebral, Oden sunk deeper and deeper into the dark side.

Oden's life revolved around drugs and music. "Hollywood in the late '60s was one of the hot spots in American music." Oden regularly visited the local clubs so he could drink in the variety of bands performing around the city. Oden spent time "traveling around to pop festivals hearing Jimi Hendrix, Janis Joplin, the Grateful Dead, Ike & Tina Turner and the Jefferson Airplane." [140]

One day Oden began to notice the presence of the local police in his neighborhood. Although Oden only sold drugs to friends and known acquaintances, he soon realized that he was on their radar and it was time to move. He and his girlfriend decided to part ways. Oden decided to move south to the small coastal community of Laguna Beach which had the reputation of being a well-known artist colony.

Laguna Beach attracted thousands of young people from the counter culture in the '60s and '70s. The hippie movement had gained popularity in San Francisco and other parts of L.A. County and young people were coming by the droves to California to get lost in the sub-culture. Both west coast cities were responsible for the birthing of a number of influential rock groups which also provided a driving force in the youth culture.

Oden lived out of his car and began to make money selling LSD. He 'cold called' customers by "walking up and down the streets chanting acid, acid" (a slang term used for the hallucinogenic drug, LSD). [141]After finding success selling drugs on the streets, Oden moved into a small hotel room. He occasionally played his guitar in a public area close to the beach and the historic Del Camino Hotel. One night, a local hippie flutist named Ron joined Oden while he was playing his guitar in public. Ron belonged to a group called the Brotherhood of Eternal Love, a loose knit group of young drug enthusiasts. The group showed devotion to Timothy Leary, their spiritual leader of sorts. [142] Leary was a former Harvard University professor who had been unceremoniously dismissed from his academic career because of extended absences from his classes. Many believed the real reason for Leary's dismissal revolved around his alleged distribution of hallucinogenic drugs to Harvard students.

Considered to be the 'high priest of LSD', Leary was a strong advocate of this controversial drug. Leary became famous for coining the phrase, "turn on, tune in and drop out" [143] and became a key player in the counterculture movement of the '60s. The famous British rock group, the Moody Blues, even wrote the song, Legend of a Mind that spoke of the mystical professor.

Oden wasted no time fitting right into the group. The Brotherhood, "believed that by doing LSD...they would change the consciousness of people, of society." [144] The group believed that distributing the hallucinogen was a way of enlightening people. The Brotherhood operated a large illegal drug network that was responsible for producing and distributing large amounts of the legendary 'orange sunshine'. The canyons east of Laguna Beach were pretty rural and consisted of small houses where the Brotherhood resided. On the spiritual dimension, the group shared the belief that "many roads lead to God." [145]

Oden Fong believed that God was One and manifested Himself in many different forms. Yet he continued to explore other religions. Oden identified mostly with Taoism because it carried a more passive spiritual philosophy than most other religions. Taoism is a combination of mysticism, poetry and philosophical reflection, [146] that he felt most comfortable with . During this time period Oden even found time to study yoga and practice meditation

Oden had been a member of the Brotherhood of Eternal Love for almost two years by the fall of 1970. Now twenty, he continued to support himself by selling LSD and other drugs besides living with a variety of roommates who passed in and out of his life.

For a long time, Oden had kept in touch with one of his old childhood friends, Lance White. On one clear day near in the fall of 1970, Oden decided to take a trip to Joshua Tree National Forest so he could trip out, camp and meditate with Lance and another friend. Late that morning, Oden found himself in the middle of the high desert snorting a mega dose of LSD. [147] Soon the 150 doses of 'orange sunshine' took their toll on Oden's body. Oden stopped breathing and his heart stopped. After a few emotionally charged minutes, Oden's friends frantically went to look for a park ranger and were convinced that their friend had died.

What Oden found "in that place of death and darkness were no angels or bright lights ... only total detachment, total darkness." [148] Oden was more terrified than he had ever been. He still had his thinking faculties but he had no awareness of being in his physical body. He was no longer physical; only spirit, as he would later describe. Within seconds, his level of fear rose beyond description. [149]

As Oden left his physical body, his soul had entered a spiritual realm. He couldn't believe what was happening to him. He didn't believe in the Bible or the Bible's explanation of Hell, but that didn't matter. Oden appeared to be in enough of hell to catch his attention.

In those moments of despair he could feel the "souls of millions, screaming out to awaken from their endless nightmare." Oden knew he was a spirit trapped forever in an endless darkness. [150] Like those souls around him, he found himself screaming in torment as well. He knew he was in trouble— and eternally lost.

For the first and only time in his life, Oden Fong had a genuine out-of-body experience. As an agnostic who did not have any strong religious convictions, he only felt fear. The utter darkness and the screaming voices were overwhelming.

Oden quickly tried to reach out for help from any possible place he thought he could find it. He was desperate, panicked and willingly would try anything and everything at this point. Oden began to cry out to the many of ascended masters he'd studied before. He called out the names of Krishna, Buddha, Meher Baba, Paramahansa Yogananda and others. Finally, Oden frantically screamed out the name of Jesus; a stranger to Oden but someone whom he admired as a great spiritual master. [151]

Suddenly "the darkness began to quake (and) there were bright flashes of light."[152] The light "continued to increase until suddenly he was awake in his body, lying on his back in the desert with a man standing above him. Oden couldn't see any details or features because there was bright light emanating from the man, so much so that the sun which was shinning above dimmed in comparison." [153]

As the image of the man stood before him,the presence became so powerful that Oden "tried to literally push his face into the sand" to escape Him. [154] He was understandably shaken and afraid. As Oden lay on his face in the sand, with his back turned to the man, he heard a loud voice say "I AM the Alpha and the Omega, the Beginning and the End." There was something peaceful and soothing about this voice. "The voice filled all the air around him. There was now no other sound but His voice." [155]

When Oden again turned back the image had disappeared and he lay there in awe at what he had just experienced. Little did he know that the words he heard were the same words that Jesus Christ had said to His friend and follower, John, more than 1900 years prior. Suddenly, Oden awoke from his state of death; unexplicitly and miraculously he had been revived. Kneeling in the sand in the hot, hazy desert, he could still see the remnants of flashes and electric charges from the stunning brightness of the image of the man. But the piercing light had disappeared.

Lance and their friend Richard returned from their futile efforts to find a park ranger and stood in front of their friend. They were shocked and stupefied to find Oden alive. Just minutes before, they had left their friend for dead! Oden returned to Laguna Canyon and tried to chalk up what had dramatically happened to him as "an LSD experience." What actually had happened? He couldn't stop asking himself this question. Oden tried to dismiss the experience but he recognized it as the most profound moment of his life.

Oden continued to occasionally use drugs but he finally quit when he realized he couldn't continue to live his life as before. Something deep down inside of him had changed. Total strangers came up to Oden and told the twenty-one-year-old man that Christ was trying to reach out to him. Oden specifically remembered one girl who walked up to him with her Bible, and said, "God is trying to show you He's real." Oden did not want to hear about this. He was overwhelmed with the whole idea. [156]

Several weeks later, one late afternoon more changes transpired as Oden and a few of his friends played their musical instruments on the lawn of their home. A friend from the Brotherhood approached Oden with a big LSD lollypop. Oden offhandedly took part of it and sat on a seat that was removed from a car and parked in front of his house. A young man named Eddie sat down beside Oden and said to him. "My boy, you look like you just took a bite out of the fruit of the knowledge of good and evil." Alarmed by Eddie's observation, Oden immediately began to contemplate that he was heading in the wrong direction in life and threw out the lollypop. [157]

Oden knew he desperately needed God's love—the love from the same God who had saved him from eternal darkness that morning in the high desert. He decided to commit his life to Jesus Christ. During the next few weeks, he started doing things he had never done before. He initiated friendships with Christians from his area and visited Calvary Chapel in Costa Mesa.

The church had a growing number of hippies attending their services. Their pastor, Chuck Smith, had selected a young man by the name of Lonnie Frisbee to serve as the church's unofficial youth leader. Lonnie impacted Oden and other young people in the area. Frisbee encouraged his new converts to share their faith with their old buddies from the Brotherhood. Oden Fong was now a part of a bigger movement that was beginning to sweep the rest of the nation. This religious revival known as the 'Jesus movement' was "a startling development for a generation that (was) constantly accused of tripping out or copping out with sex, drugs and violence ... embracing the most persistent symbol of purity, selflessness and brotherly love ..." These born-again Christians were "afire with Pentecostal passion for sharing their vision with others." [158]

Oden and his new Christian buddies shared their new found faith with their old friends from the neighborhood. By the spring of 1971 Oden decided it was time to completely break away from his old group. He resigned his membership from the Brotherhood and turned in his leather strapped pendant, a symbol of one's allegiance to the group.

Within weeks, Oden started regularly attending Bible studies. Drawn to the church's worship services, he sensed the power and presence of God.[159] Oden felt inspired by the church's music concerts where he heard the church's first contemporary Christian band, Love Song.

Calvary Chapel met weekly in a small building that seated only around 200 people. Although crowded with hippies, he could feel the powerful presence of God. The church also regularly held baptisms at Pirate's Cove near Corona Del Mar. One such baptism was described by a writer from Time Magazine. "Under the setting sun, several hundred converts waded into the cold Pacific, patiently waiting their turn for the rite. On the cliffs above, hundreds more watched.... As the baptisms ended, the crowd slowly climbed a narrow stairway up the cliff singing a moving Lord's Prayer in the twilight." [160]

Music was an integral part of Calvary Chapel's worship service. Pastor Chuck's willingness to provide a platform for these converts to share their musical gifts with the rest of his young congregation proved to be a novel idea. Oden openly shared, "If you showed some talent, you would most likely be invited to share again." [161]

Even before his conversion, Oden had played guitar with his friend Pedro Buford. By the end of 1971 Oden considered joining Pedro's band, Mustard Seed. Over the course of the next four years, the group took on a variety of different members. The band eventually put together a number of contemporary Christian ballads and was renamed Mustard Seed Faith. Pedro and Oden's band experienced success because it played music that met the spiritual needs of their generation. Mustard Seed Faith logged thousands of miles each year touring throughout the U.S.

Maranatha Music record label released the band's first, long awaited album, Sail on Sailor in 1975. The release opened up brand new venues for the band and provided financial support. Playing 350 concerts a year took its toll on each of the members of the band, causing them to eventually break up. Despite this, the band's members still maintain their friendship with each other. In 1980 the band recorded a performance for a "limited edition" reunion album. [162] After Mustard Seed Faith disbanded in 1977, Oden decided to pursue a solo music career. Jonathan David Brown persuaded Maranatha Music to sponsor a solo album featuring the twenty-seven year old musician. Oden's first solo project, Come for the Children, was released in 1978 (Music notes), the same year that Oden became an ordained minister.

Oden's new record rekindled public interest in his music. For a few years, Oden toured around the country, but somehow it felt different. The innocence of the early days had vanished and the motives of the Christian music business had changed. Ultimately Oden became disillusioned and made the decision to retire (in 1982) from his full time music ministry.

Over the next eleven years, Oden Fong found himself in a variety of occupations ranging from general manager of his father's restaurant chain, Ah Fongs, to an administrative Outreach Director for Calvary Chapel, Costa Mesa. Oden took on the responsibility of working with his home church in Costa Mesa and their 450+ affiliate churches around the world.

Oden's passion for the ministry continued after his ordination, and by 2003 Pastor Fong decided to start a new church in Huntington Beach, California. The Poiema Christian Fellowship is located in the same community where he lives with his wife, Samantha and their three sons, Maxwell, Jack and Seth.

God is not finished with Oden Fong! Oden will never, ever forget that pivotal moment when Jesus clearly spoke to him and pulled him back from the edge of Hell. It seems clear by his story that we all are a work in progress. Until our last dying breath, we all have opportunities to touch lives around us. Oden is now doing that by serving the people of his community, reaching out to them with the same love that delivered him so many years ago in a high desert at Joshua Tree National Park.

Oden can be contacted by email at odenfong@aol.com.

Chapter 7

Brian Welch KoRn's Former Lead Guitarist's Radical Transformation

"Music is what feelings sound like."
~Author Unknown

No one knows the reality of this quote better than Brian Welch. Although there are some detours in life, if we follow the signs, we can usually find our way back to the main road. This is what Brian Welch did!

Welch was born during the tumultuous era of the 1970s when youth questioned parental values and authority. Peace signs, flower power, and Vietnam headlines were indelibly etched into the times. Much of the dissatisfaction with the status quo and search for meaning in life became songs during this period.

As Welch told Rolling Stone Magazine, "When I was thirteen, I was hanging around this family that was very peaceful – they hardly ever fought. They told me about Jesus ... I drifted away from them. Puberty hit, and I got into trouble." [163]

Life was problematic during his middle and high school years. Brian described himself as "shy, weak, and someone who was made fun of a lot." His brother, Jeff, remembers that his younger sibling "was really reclusive in high school." [164] He chose to seek refuge in his music.

Welch began playing the guitar at eleven and spent an inordinate amount of time practicing. Through his music, he found a place to fit in and we all know that those teenage years are all about finding your niche. For the next several years Brian "started getting into music ... it (music) just made me feel like I belonged somewhere, you know?" [165] He was certainly gifted and "had an ear for music. (He) was figuring out heavy metal songs by Ted Nugent, Ozzy Osbourne, and Queen really quick the first couple of years." [166]

Brian's unique ability to play the guitar brought requests from his brother's friends. It soon became evident that he had definite talent. The kind of music that captured his interest took him into the next step: experimentation with drugs. He told Rolling Stones' reporter, Alex Mar, "I started really drinking and partying when I was sixteen." These habits (doing drugs and drinking) continued to follow him during the peaks and valleys of much of his young life. Brian's father, Phil, told one publication that he was always concerned about his son's drug use; but as many teenagers, Brian denied he even had a problem.

During his teens, Brian met and befriended some of the future members of the rock group that ultimately was to make him rich and famous. His determination and dedication to music gained him respect. After graduation, Welch spent hours jamming in his parent's garage with some of his future band mates. "Guitarist James 'Munky' Shaffer, bassist Reginald 'Fieldy' Arvizu, drummer David Silveria and guitarist Welch initially formed the musical group that captured the attention of youth around the world. Jonathan Davis (from the group Sexart) was asked to be their lead singer.

Brian's band actually got their start as the Bakersfield, Ca. based metal band, LAPD." [167]

The band moved into a tiny house in Los Angeles, giving them increased exposure from fans that frequented music clubs around the city. They were followed by numerous groupies who were mesmerized by their unique, hard sound and were ultimately discovered by representatives of the music industry. The band was called KoRn, and supported a sound that Billboard Magazine once described as "alternative metal."

"It was near Death Valley where Welch and fellow guitarist James Shaffer developed the groundbreaking band's heavy, growling metal influenced sound using seven-string guitars." [168] That combination along with the band's lyrics spoke of the alienation, pain, anger and rage of youth, and created a ground swell of support.

KoRn signed with the Epic/Immortal label and released their first CD/album in 1994. Welch basked in success and immediately began a frenetic touring schedule by opening for well-known acts such as Megadeth, Ozzy Osbourne, and Marilyn Manson. As the opening act in the tour, KoRn benefited by playing before audiences that craved their dark, hard, and even sinister representation of life.

Welch celebrated when KoRn's first album eventually went gold and sold more than 500,000 copies (RIAA). The accomplishment was stellar for a group that had recently been unknown. KoRn followed their first album/CD with the release of Life is Peachy in 1996, Follow the Leader in 1998 and Issues in 1999. [169]

The group KoRn routinely ignited controversy. A principal from a Michigan High School suspended a student for wearing a KoRn T-shirt, calling the band's music, "indecent, vulgar and obscene."[170] To add to their dark-side image, the group's lead singer (Jonathan Davis) bought the Volkswagen that convicted serial killer Ted Bundy had once owned. KoRn had toured with Marilyn Manson, "whose violent sexual and anti-religious stage antics included burning Bibles and drinking urine which had riled parents across the nation." [171] Many parents also became wary of the explicit lyrics of some of KoRn's songs. The RIAA placed the "Parental Advisory – Explicit Content" label on a number of KoRn's CDs including three of their first studio releases.

Welch dreamed of reaching stardom. He wanted to become rich and famous, but drugs and the fast life of a rock group were taking their toll. The lead guitarist admitted to several publications that he sometimes suffered from depression and could see that his life was spinning out of control.

For thousands of fans, KoRn continued as a voice for their generation's expression of anger and frustration with society. In January and February of 1997, the group played to audiences in Germany, Spain, France, the UK and the Netherlands. In just five short years, KoRn went from playing small clubs to world-wide fame.

Brian eventually married his long time girlfriend, Rebekah. Their marriage started off on rocky ground as both abused drugs and alcohol in excessive quantities. Rebekah, however, did give birth to a beautiful baby girl, Jennea not long afterward. The birth of his daughter caused Brian to see the need to give up drugs, but he couldn't cure his cravings.

KoRn performed before the biggest audience of their career at Woodstock '99. Some of the era's biggest rock stars, including Metallica, The Dave Mathews Band, Red Hot Chili Peppers, Megadeth, Ice Cube, Jewel, Sheryl Crow, Elvis Costello and Lim Bizket also performed at the mega-music event held at a former Air Force base in New York from July 23-25, 1999.[172]

Woodstock '99 also marked the 30th anniversary of the historic Woodstock music festival of 1969 in New York State and included several of the original Woodstock performers. Considered one of the most gifted guitar players of his generation, Brian recognized Hendrix' legendary guitar playing ability. In a concert appearance a year after his famous Woodstock '69 appearance, Jimi Hendrix asked a San Diego audience, "What is truth?"[173] Regrettably, it appears the gifted musician might not have found an answer. Jimi Hendrix died in London, England on September 18, 1970 from asphyxiation most likely related to drug and alcohol abuse. One publication (Bio.com) labeled the cause of death as "drug related complications."[174] Hendrix died the same year that Brian Welch was born. Thirty years later Brian and the rock world were to celebrate another Woodstock festival.

Woodstock '99 turned into a wild experience for Brian and his wife, Rebekah. Brian told CNN's Paula Zahn, "We played in front of 200,000 people, and they were all going nuts. And we were like, wow." Brian and his wife "dined on ecstasy, cocaine, and meth the entire week, including on the private jet flights there and back with

Limp Bizkit and Ice Cube." [175] It wasn't until he came back from New York that Brian started to grasp that their lives were spiraling out of control. Welch reminded himself, "I had $3 million in cash sitting in the bank, all the cars I wanted, a $200,000 pool, nannies, the nicest house, real estate in California. I was miserable." [176]

The drug use, the arguments with his wife Rebekah, and the bouts with depression were escalating. Everything crystallized one night when Brian found himself over his wife, her blood covering his fist. He knew he couldn't continue living this way. Brian's wife left and his marriage fell apart. Reality struck him in the face — much like his own bloody fist. He was now a single parent of their little girl, Jennea. His world was rocked when Rebekah "failed to attend the court date concerning Jennea (and) Welch gained full custody." [177] These new pressures in his personal life led him to an even greater dependency on drugs. He could not cope with being a celebrity rock star and a full-time dad.

Instinctively, Welch knew that things had to change. Every time he tried to escape the cycle of drugs and depression; his efforts fell short and his melancholy deepened. Life on the road, along with the band's packed concert schedule continued to make life untenable. Brian later admitted that he "just didn't care ... I was really into my depression." [178]

One day the young father heard his five-year-old daughter sing his band's controversial, X-rated song entitled 'A.D.I.D.A.S.' and reality set in. Brian knew the controversial lyrics all too well. "All day I dream about sex, all day I dream about f—ing ... I don't know your f—ing name, so what, let's f—." [179] As a young parent, he felt shame. Something deep inside of him welled up and he knew he couldn't allow this negative influence in his young daughter's life. He began to panic until a series of curious incidents occurred that clearly revealed the fingerprints of a loving God.

Brian decided to reach out to a Christian friend. He remembered as a young boy "asking Jesus into his heart ... remembering a presence of peace and love that had embraced him as a youth." [180] Brian read a simple Bible verse he found in Matthew 11 that had a lasting effect on him. "Come to me, all you who are weary and burdened, and I will give you rest." [181] The life-changing words continued, "Take my yoke upon you and learn from me, for I am gentle and humble in heart, and you will find rest for your soul. For my yoke is easy and my burden is light." [182] The reality check of those words drew the young rock star to a real and heartfelt new understanding about the God of Heaven who had gifted him with his musical ability. Brian knew he needed to turn to God for any real change in his life to take place and to stick. He knew he needed a relationship with the only One who could bring him peace.

It became evident that a powerful force was leading Brian to make a profound shift in his life. Brian decided to attend a church in Bakersfield, CA. Imagine how surreal it must have been for the members of that church to see this heavy-metal rock star quietly enter their sanctuary! What they did not know was how tormented the poor man had become. They could not see the demons hounding him, nor his debilitating depression pushing him closer to ending his life. When he returned home after the church service, he spoke these sincere words from the pit of his pain, "Jesus, if you are real, take this stuff away from me. Make me a good person again, take away my suicidal thoughts. Make me want to live again." [183]

God began to answer the young musician's prayers and his thoughts of depression and suicide lessened. He sought solitude in a hotel where he prayed and experienced his first drug-free week in years. Welch told a CNN television audience that while undergoing detoxification, he prayed and simply said, "Okay God, I want you to strip this (drug addiction) from me. You're the Healer, take this from me." [184]

Brian reported, "Within a couple of weeks, I was off drugs and feeling good which is unheard of when you're a speed addict … I had been filled with anger, confusion, hate, selfishness, greed, you name it. When God revealed Himself to me, it was a supernatural peace and love that was so far higher and beyond anything you can experience on earth." [185]

Anyone who knows anything about hard drug use knows that true stories like this certainly border on the miraculous. Brian's speedy recovery from drug abuse is a glorious testimony of the awesome power of God. It is a clear demonstration of what God can do in a person's life. Clearly, the God of the Bible is alive today!

Brian's firsthand experience of God's power resulted in his decision to make a public announcement of his conversion in front of his friends and acquaintances in Valley Bible Fellowship on February 27, 2005. Brian was "wearing blue jeans and a T-shirt, with his signature long, curly hair in his face ...."[186] "He told a packed church audience in his hometown that he "thought (he) had it all, everything that (he) thought was important when (he) was a kid – money, fame, pretty women." [187]

Lifting up his Bible, the musician said, "This is the book of life right here ... It's not about religion, it's not about this church, it's not about me." [188] Instead the professional guitarist found the real meaning of life in Jesus Christ. Convinced that Jesus had performed a miracle in his restoration, Brian decided to join the church's pastor in their regular pilgrimage to Israel. Weeks later, Welch was baptized in the Jordan River by Valley Bible Fellowship's Pastor, Ron Vietti.

He felt strongly that God led him in a decision to leave KoRn. The choice and subsequent announcement to leave the group created a media frenzy. Cameras from MTV, CNN, and some local network affiliates followed the professional musician even on his spiritual visit to the shores of Israel's Jordan River.

Overwhelmed by joy over his new found transformation, Brian's outlook on life changed dramatically. Welch's conversion to Christianity has since served to encourage a whole new generation of youth. Brian's desire to find peace in life was genuine even though many of his fans and friends questioned his motives.

When Brian left KoRn, he walked away from a Virgin Records' contract extension offer that had not yet been announced. The decision cost the guitarist millions of dollars. Nevertheless, Welch was convinced he couldn't put a price on the tranquility he had found in his new relationship with Christ. Criticism was to be expected from those who couldn't understand but it had no impact on him as he pursued this new relationship.

Brian's quest for personal peace and his subsequent deliverance from drug dependency has resulted in a total makeover of the former musician's life. Today, Brian continues to play guitar and play professionally before new audiences and old fans as he hopes to touch the lives of many young people as well. His purpose is to reach his generation with the message of hope and agape love that only the Risen Savior can provide. Brian continues to share the Good News of Christ all across the country. In April, 2010 Brian shared his dramatic Christian conversion in an appearance with Jennea at the New Generation Church (www.NewGenerationFellowship.net) in San Antonio, Texas. According to Senior Pastor Joseph Garza both are eager to share the grace and love that the God had shown them since that life changing day in 2005. Brian continues spreading the truth he has discovered in the pages of the Bible with his fans from around the world.

Brian Welch's autobiography, Save Me from Myself, (2007) and another newer book, Washed by the Blood (2008) are both published by Harper Collins. Brian is currently working on several new music projects. He has already released several recordings and continues to create music that reflects his new relationship with Christ. To help support Brian's ministry and his ongoing effort to reach people with the Good News of Christ, you can visit his website at www. BrianHeadWelch.net.

Regardless of your position in life, no matter how far you have wandered, or what you have done, God is waiting for you with open arms. The same God of the Bible is available to each of us today, ready to reach out and show His great love. He never leaves us; but we leave Him. So, it's time for each of us to make the decision to come home to Him.

Chapter 8

William J. Murray From Atheist to God's Friend

M ost of us are influenced by what we were taught as children. When we become able to sift ideas and deliberate for ourselves, we can disengage from any negative patterns. That is exactly what William Murray accomplished.

For much of his early life, William (Bill) Murray's identity was closely intertwined with that of his mother, Madalyn Murray O'Hare.

Madalyn Mays drew her first breath in Pennsylvania in 1919. Prior to America's entrance into the Second World War, she married John Roths and they both enlisted. Madalyn joined the US Army and John joined the US Marines. By mid-1945 Madalyn found herself in an affair with a young Army Air Corps officer by the name of William J. Murray, Jr. Both Madalyn and William Jr. were already married which complicated matters. William, a devout Catholic, had no intention of leaving his wife; even after he discovered Madalyn's pregnancy.

Devastated by Murray's abandonment, Madalyn blamed the church. She became convinced that the Catholic Church and the Pope played a significant role in this rejection.

When Madalyn's husband, John Roths, returned from the Pacific, he began searching for his estranged wife. His persistence led him to Haysville, Ohio, where Madalyn had purchased a small farmhouse in the rural community. Roths found out that his wife of four years was pregnant but still offered to stay. Madalyn responded to his offer by filing for divorce. On May 25th, 1946 Madelyn Roths gave birth to her first child, William (Bill) Joseph Murray and decided to change her name to Madalyn Murray in spite of her lover's rejection. At first, Madalyn found it difficult to support her family and had to take on variety of jobs just to survive. She lived with relatives including her brother (Uncle Irv) and William's grandfather, John.[189]

Eventually Madalyn couldn't meet the payments on the farmhouse, and so she and the rest of her family decided to move to Texas. Once there, they gained some financial stability when Madalyn secured a job as a county probation officer.

Six-year-old William and the family again moved but this time across the country to Baltimore, MD. The prospects of a possible business venture with other relatives lured his mother to the city. William's eighth birthday was celebrated with a visit from his birth father who gave his son a model airplane fashioned after the plane he flew during World War II. Unfortunately, that was the last time William ever saw him.

By 1954, William's half-brother, Jon Garth was born. William couldn't recall any details about Jon's father because he only visited their home one other time before Jon's birth.

After moving to Baltimore, William's mother became involved with the local chapter of the Socialist Labor Party. Young William overheard daily arguments between his grandfather and mother and they troubled him. While he could not understand all of the political mumbo-jumbo, he somehow knew that his mother lacked respect for grandfather's way of thinking. He was left alone a great deal and his mother's apathy towards him only soured their strained relationship.

William's mother became intrigued with the idea of immigrating to the Soviet Union. She became so consumed with this prospect that she even traveled to France one summer for a month. Once in Paris, Madalyn attempted to persuade the embassy's personnel to grant her entrance into the Soviet state. After weeks of frustrating, non-productive dialogue with the Soviet Embassy officials, her money ran out and she returned to the U.S.

Upon arriving back to Maryland, Madalyn informed her oldest son that he'd have to enroll in school the next day. William recalled in his book, *My Life without God*, that this "first day back at school would change (his) life forever." [190]

The next morning Madalyn decided to drive Bill to school so she could tell school officials about the late enrollment. When Madalyn walked down the school's hallway on that fateful day, she observed something that deeply troubled her. She saw students in class reciting the pledge of allegiance. Deeply opposed to any public religious expression, she didn't like the phrase "under God." As Madalyn and her son walked past another class room, she asked William if prayer and religious recitals were daily occurrences at Woodbourne. William responded in the affirmative. Continuing down the hall, they both passed yet another classroom where a group of children were reciting the Lord's Prayer.

William's mother became incensed. She decided to confront a school district employee over the occurrences. She expressed her opposition to the prayers and religious recitals by lacing her criticism with profanities. The school counselor couldn't understand why Murray so vehemently opposed something that most considered as positive. Years later, William pointed out in his book, *My Life without God*, that the counselor may have given his mother an idea when he suggested that she could sue the school if she disagreed. [191]

Determined to do something about the religious expression, she gave her fourteen-year-old boy instructions about keeping a written log detailing any religious activity at the school each day. Bill recalled years latter that up to that point, his mother had shown little interest in her son's daily school activity. But now, all that changed.

William's absences from school were not permitted, especially during the daily pledge of allegiance or prayer recitals. Woodbourne set its own ultimatum and confrontation loomed ahead.

Young Murray's teenage years were anything but normal. Bill became weary of all the arguments and the unwanted stress. His mother's battle with the school district escalated to new heights of rage. The release of a news story in the area's local newspaper, The Baltimore Sun, detailed Murray's fight with the school over prayer.

It attracted interest in other area news services as well. Radio and local affiliates from various television networks started lining up at the Murray household to get their take of the story. Nevertheless, Madalyn became oblivious to the pain and unwanted attention these stories caused William. The kids picked on Bill and fist fights broke out.

In the heat of his mother's clash with the school district, Madalyn sought advice from American Civil Liberties Union (ACLU) attorney Fred Weisgal. The ACLU has a long history of attempting "to expunge America of its affinity to Christianity and strip our society of its Judeo-Christian touchstone and foundation." [192] However, Madalyn decided to dump the ACLU when she "learned that all financial donations ... would go to them."[193] Instead, Madalyn joined forces with her attorney Leonard Kerpelman to file their case against the school district. [194]

Ultimately the state's Attorney General's decision sided with the school district. However, the ruling did allow people who objected to prayers or religious recitals in school the right to remove themselves from the classroom during the activity. While Madalyn won the right to excuse her son from these activities, she still felt that her own rights as an atheist had been denied. They appealed the case to the city's Superior Court. When the Baltimore court decided to dismiss the case, Madalyn's attorney forwarded the case to the Maryland Court of Appeals.

Young Murray sought solace in his relationship with his grandfather, John. There were times when the distraught young teenager considered running away. The pressures which Bill endured from home and school continued. By the fall of 1961, William couldn't wait to enter a new high school where he could make a fresh start. He enrolled in Baltimore's Polytechnic Institute.

His mother's income was derived from activists from all over the world. Support for her cause had grown remarkably resulting in financial freedom for first time in her life.[195] Clearly, Madalyn's allegiance to the case attracted support. The Appeals Court ruled in favor of the school district but only with a very close 4-3 decision in April 1962. That same year, Madalyn appealed to the United States Supreme

Court. The court decided it would consolidate Murray's case (Murray vs. Curtlett) with Abington School District vs. Schempp. The court would hear the Murray case on February 26, 1963. That year turned out to be a momentous year for his family. (In January, Bill's grandfather died at the age of sixty-nine and his grandson was grief stricken over the loss.)

The day arrived and on February 26,1963, attorney Kerpelman, William and Madalyn Murray entered the hall of the United States Supreme Court in Washington, DC. Kerpelman argued their case in front of nine Supreme Court justices. In his arguments for the court, the attorney defended Madalyn's son's right of separation of church and state. Justice Potter Stewart questioned the attorney's constitutional interpretation of religion's place in the public school. While a number of state attorney generals defended the action of the Baltimore school district, no supporting amicus briefs were filed by any Christian organizations whatsoever. Even the National Council of Churches supported the Murray's case. How could this be? A country founded on faith had let a good defense slip away.

By June the Supreme Court made its final decision. SCOTUS reversed the Maryland decision that was earlier decided against the Murrays. By an 8-1 margin, the court voted to rule that prayer and Bible reading were unconstitutional in public schools. Centuries of tradition and allegiance to Christian precepts in America's public schools were wiped out by this one 1963 decision. Madalyn was simply elated! Life magazine responded by labeling William's mother as the most hated woman in America. [195]

All William Murray wanted to do was put all this behind him so that he could finish school. Girls were on his radar and by seventeen William had his first girlfriend, Susan. While Susan's parents opposed the relationship, their daughter maintained that they abused her. Eventually she moved into the Murray household.

Marriage is No Escape

As William turned eighteen, Susan's parents took legal action against him. They charged Murray with enticing their daughter to live with him and corrupting her with his atheistic beliefs. The young couple decided to get married after William found out that Susan was pregnant. The couple thought that by escaping to New York, William's legal problems would disappear. Upon his return to Baltimore, Bill found himself on the way to city jail.

Kerpelman posted bail and this time his mother decided it best for her family to relocate. She pronounced that the predominately Catholic city of Baltimore was probably not the best place for them to live. Based, in part, on a friend's advice, the family moved to Hawaii. She believed that the fiftieth state would be more tolerant towards atheists. [196]

Madalyn still controlled the family's money and Bill's life as well. Bill and Susan had a baby girl and named her Robin. William's legal problems continued to follow him to Hawaii. He realized that he could either respond to the warrants or move elsewhere. He chose to move, although he felt uneasy about leaving his young bride and baby with his extended family.

No one could foresee the bizarre events ahead. William went from living on a dope ranch in a remote Mexican countryside, to being in trouble with Mexican authorities because of a delinquent hotel bill. Eventually he grew tired of running and finally gave himself up. When he returned to the states, the police located him in West Virginia and took him back to Baltimore to serve time in the county jail. Attorney Kerpelman decided to help his old friend; Bill entered an innocent plea and the charges were eventually dropped.

By the time William returned to Hawaii, Susan had already filed for divorce. Bill found himself attracted to new sights, new experiences and new people. He enjoyed smoking pot, drinking alcohol and getting into all sorts of mischief. He had eyes for a young girl by the name of Linda and left for California with her by his side.

In California William found work in San Francisco in the advertising field. By the following year (1966) William had to fly back to Honolulu for a few days to finalize his divorce with Susan as well as bring his daughter, Robin, back to live in the bay area with him.

It quickly became apparent to Bill that it would be impossible for him to care for the child. He quit his job and left for Austin with his daughter. Once in Texas, William left Robin in his mother's care until things turned around. For the next thirteen weeks, Bill bummed around the country with Linda. They ended up in Boston where Bill worked as an undercover agent.

"By the end of 1967 I moved back to Hawaii working for an airline company," Bill recalled years later. [197] About a year later he enlisted in the U.S. Army, desiring to enroll in the Army's flight program. Once again William had to deal with the negative impact of his mother's dubious affiliations. Bill was tired of being punished for his mother's behavior. [198] William was able to complete two years of military service and did receive an honorable discharge from the U.S. Army. (By this time Madalyn had married Richard O'Hair, a former FBI employee and WWII veteran.)

Bill headed back to Honolulu to start his own Taxi Cab Company. Bill's company grew to a fleet of five taxis that he successfully operated in Hawaii's capitol city. William sold the company in 1975. He again decided to move back to the mainland, this time to Denver, Colorado where he set up a printing business. Despite the success of the business Bill was enticed by a proposal from his mother regarding a business venture with her back in Texas. Essentially Madalyn promised to give her son a sizable amount of new business if he would move his printing operation to Texas.

After just six months in the Lone Star State, Bill started regretting relocating near his mother. He was suffering from severe mood swings and found himself turning to alcohol.

During America's bicentennial William decided to make a run for a US Congressional seat in his state of Texas. Bill lost his election bid, with the Republican candidate earning more than 45% of the district's vote. While involved in all kinds of business and political ventures, he still had time for romance and William married his longtime secretary and companion, Valerie, in 1977.

(Meanwhile, Madalyn continued her rabid involvement in atheist causes.) Married life was good this time and William and Valerie welcomed a daughter, Jade, into their family. Again, Bill decided to move. He traveled with Valerie and Jade to Tucson, Arizona. His mother had already sent his daughter, Robin, to Tucson so she could attend a boarding school. This move put William closer to Robin.

On the Road to Recovery

Always searching for his niche, Bill again tried another line of business and this time he chose a book store but it did not last long. William became convinced that he needed to get back into the airline business. His past experience in the airline industry helped him land a job with Commutair as their Passenger Services Director. With Valerie and Jade in his life, Bill began to get serious about dealing with his drinking problem.

Bill learned that the twelve-step program offered a good chance of overcoming his addiction. He decided to attend their regular meetings. Valerie was working full time, and her arduous schedule caused a severe strain on the couple's relationship. His anger spiraled out of control, and one fateful day in 1979, Bill became so enraged that he shot a 'warning shot' at his own doorway after suspecting another man had entered his home. Unfortunately for Murray, the man on the other side of the doorway was a police officer.

This incident, along with some of the other troubles from his past, caused Bill to ask himself some serious questions about life. On a whim, William started reading a book about the Apostle Luke. On January 24, 1980 Bill recalled experiencing a "nightmare of unmentionable horror." He dreamed that he "was sliced in half by a mighty, gleaming sword of gold and silver. A great winged angel stood with the sword in his hand. The blade of the sword pointed down, making it resemble a cross. On the sword's hilt were inscribed the words "IN HOC SIGNO VINCE." The tip of the sword's blade touched an open Bible." [200] The inscribed words translate "in this sign you will conquer" – pointing to the pages of the Bible. This event had a profound and lasting effect on Bill's life.

Finding Christ

How ironic that William's search for truth and peace brought him to the pages of the Bible. This was the same inspired book that he and his mother had fought so hard to keep out of the public school system seventeen years earlier! The next morning he woke up in his apartment with a yearning to locate a Bible. William found one in a small store not far from his home.

After he read the book of Luke from the New Testament, William Murray knew his fight with God was over. That day he fell to his knees; asked God to forgive him of all his sins and he asked Jesus Christ to take control of his life. Bill Murray finally became a free man! Within days, he started noticing dramatic changes in his life. He understood the damage he had caused to those around him. It was on that day that William finally began to understand the power of forgiveness.

William sent a letter to the people of Baltimore (Maryland) apologizing for his part in the famous Supreme Court case of 1963, and the moral and spiritual chaos it brought to America. Over the course of the next few years, Bill spoke at over 400 churches. He also gave numerous interviews addressing his story and his new life as a Christian.

William's metamorphosis affected his marriage. In 1982 Valeri filed for divorce, and in 1983 she asked William to take custody of their daughter, Jade. Bill was overjoyed to have Jade back in his life again.

As for his mother, Madalyn, William hadn't maintained any contact with her for years. He experienced genuine sadness that his brother Joh and daughter Robin had turned away from him also. Both called him a traitor because he had accepted Christ. Author Ted Dracos quoted his mother as saying she had decided to "repudiate him entirely and completely for now and all times..."[201] Madalyn's organization, American Atheists, represented the face of atheism in America. Her son, now a committed Christian, became a polarizing figure for her.

After dedicating his life to Christ, William found time to set up a commercial Bible printing company in the Soviet Union in addition to arranging evangelistic tours to that country. Murray's personal outreach to former atheists was seeing profound results.

In September of 1995 his mother re-entered his life once again but this time, under tragic circumstances. William received a call from a reporter asking him questions about his mother's strange disappearance. His brother, Jon Garth, and Robin had also disappeared from their home in Austin, Texas. He could only speculate. William hadn't communicated with his mother in many years. His mother was predictably unpredictable. With little evidence to fall back on, William filed a missing person's police report. After little cooperation from the Austin police department, he contacted his friend, Congressman Dick Armey, who got the FBI involved in the case.

By the end of the decade William was living in the state of Virginia and years had passed since he was informed of his mother's disappearance. Eventually William received the long awaited call. An agent assigned to the case told him that his mother, his brother and daughter had been found murdered. They were viciously tortured and their bodies were found mutilated at the crime scene. "The dismembered bodies of Madalyn Murray O'Hair, Jon Murray and Robin Murray were found in January of 2000 in Camp Wood, Texas." [202] At this point William could only hope that, in their last moments, his family members had given their lives to a forgiving, and loving Savior.

Today William J. Murray is the chairman of the Religious Freedom Coalition in Washington, DC. Mr. Murray continues to work for the rights of Christians in America and persecuted Christians around the world. Murray tirelessly represents Christians abroad, especially those who are tragically persecuted in the Middle East. His organization works diligently to minister to the whole person by providing various forms of aid to our persecuted brothers and sisters in Christ. You can support his work by contacting him at his website: www. religiousfreedomcoalition.org.

Even today, William is understandably reluctant to talk about his past. However, it is clear by his intense story that a loving and gracious God reached out and made Himself known to William Joseph Murray. All of us have the free will to make our own decision about God. But William's story clearly sends us the message that the only thing that separates us from God's love is our own free will. William found the peace he was looking for. You too, can find rest by entering into a relationship with the Savior of the world, Jesus Christ.

[Author's note: The complete and fascinating story of William J. Murray's early life and conversion can be found in his autobiography: My Life Without God, 1992]

Mickey Mantle, Bobby Richardson and Whitey Ford

Bobby Richardson, 1960 World Series MVP

Mt. Vernon (Virginia)

Statue of General Baron Von Steuben

Steve McQueen (4th from right – top row) at Boy's Republic

Steve McQueen's star on side walk (Hollywood, CA.)

Ruben De La Torre

Ronald & Nancy Reagan, 'Peggy' Goldwater, Jim & Joanne Lambert

Oden Fong

Supreme Court Building (Washington, DC)

Steve McQueen's last home (in Santa Paula, CA.)

Michael Glatze

Darren Carrington

Maria McKee & Brian Maclean

Elizabeth McKee

Brenda and Raymond MacKillop

Pat White

Jim and Joanne Lambert (1939)

The home of Officer Bullit in Steve McQueen's popular 1968 movie (that was filmed in San Francisco)

Chaplain Max Foresman

Adina & Frank Friesen

Hewitt Hall – Linfield College

Stephen Schrater

Tim McGill

Nick Burt

Chapter 9

Annie Meadows Former Witch Sees "The Light" and Now Sings for God

Where people are born and raised has a lot to do with who they become. To understand someone, you have to imagine the backdrop of their early years. The provincial mid-west of Cairo, Illinois bordered the state of Kentucky on the Mason-Dixon Line and provides a rich history. The riverboat town became incorporated in the 1800s and is on the confluence of the Ohio and Mississippi Rivers where Fort Defiance is located. The historic military fort where the town is located was once commanded by Civil War General Ulysses S. Grant. The intriguing community of Cairo is even mentioned in Samuel L. Clemens's famous book, The Adventures of Tom Sawyer.

Annie Meadows was the youngest of four children born to Carmon Alton Meadows and his wife, Aileen. Her father, Al, was an industrious mechanic and a dedicated provider for his family. Annie's mother, Aileen, took on the traditional role of housewife. Aileen took great pride in raising her four children. Annie's parents were Christians, and attended both the local Catholic and Baptist churches. Annie's childhood days bubbled with fun and frivolity. However, she did have an experience in her early years that was to have an ominous effect on her life for years to come.

When Annie was five or six years old she was invited to play an Ouija board game. She soon became so fascinated that she engaged with it regularly. She sought every opportunity to indulge herself in her new hobby and learn everything about the board. Her parents were unaware of the dangers of the occult and did not fully understand the possibility of evil or dark spirits that their child could be exposed to. [203]

The earliest known origin of the Ouija board dates back to China before the time of Christ. Experts believe the board to be a tool to tap into the spirit world, and when Annie played the game she discovered a special power she hadn't experienced before. Intrigued by its mystery and magic the Ouija's access to the other side mysteriously beckoned to her. The local library became her favorite haunt as Annie spent hours devouring books on witchcraft, even though she was still learning how to read. As Annie's knowledge of the occult grew, so did her skills in black magic. Annie's fascination with the occult allowed her to delve into spiritual topics well beyond her years.

Despite her obsession with the occult, God was still very real to her in elementary school. When socializing with classmates at playtime during school, she usually insisted that everyone pray first, making her appear odd to some of the kids. Annie even showed her reverence to God by kneeling at her bed to pray before she went to sleep at night. Annie also had a deep respect for her father, Carmon. She remembered her father once telling her while sitting on the front porch together, "Everything you see, everything that is created tells you that there is a God." Deep down inside Annie knew her father was right. But the lure of magic and the mysteries of the spirit world continued to entice her as she kept her life in the occult a secret. [204]

While attending Camelot High School Annie found herself living a double life. On the surface she fit in with her classmates, but inside she realized the difference. As she became more and more caught up in the occult, she started predicting future events of friends and acquaintances around her. Annie recalled telling one girl friend that a fire would start in her room in three days. When Annie's prediction came true in exactly three days, her friend became frightened.

Just dabbling in the occult wasn't enough anymore; and so Annie embraced her identity as a witch. Like all teenagers, she became very good at keeping secrets and even her own parents had no idea how deeply involved she had become in black magic. Annie didn't join a coven, she just thought she had been born to be a witch. As Annie later explained, "It was who I was becoming." [205] Even though she loved her family and appreciated her natural talent for music, Annie realized that the depth of involvement in the occult would not allow her to just walk away or give up.

The use of Tarot cards and fortune telling were a few of her cultic practices. Meadows experienced an adrenaline rush when she used Tarot cards and she liked it! She relished exercising her skills as a witch even more. She viewed herself as a strong willed and independent woman who had nothing to apologize for, and furthermore believed that her powers were completely under her control.

As Annie's immersion in the occult became more pronounced, she started experimenting with marijuana and other illegal drugs. By the time she graduated from Camelot High, she had become isolated from her peers. She decided to enroll in nearby Southern Illinois University (SIU). However, after attending the university for several semesters, Annie decided to change course to pursue her dream of becoming a professional singer. Meadows sold what little she had and left for Hollywood to establish a career in music and acting.

Annie Meadows had always been a uniquely gifted singer. She had performed in rock groups back home, and she wanted to see if she could make it as a professional vocalist. After arriving in Hollywood, she quickly found herself in a difficult situation, as she discovered she was pregnant by her former boyfriend. In her conversations with her boyfriend, it was made clear that he didn't want anything to do with Annie or her unexpected problem.

Desperation set it! With her confirmed pregnancy, the clinic counselor described Meadow's thirteen-week old fetus as a blob. The counselor explained that her baby had not fully formed and couldn't be a human being. He told Annie that "having an abortion was in her best interest" reminding her that she "had her whole life ahead of her." [206]

As a young girl, she had no facts on abortion. While at this California clinic, she remembered being surrounded by fifteen patients who bragged of numerous abortions they had already undergone. Some of the patients appeared to be as young as fifteen. Shock does not describe what she felt when she heard how some of the girls admitted to being there five or six times.

It took years for Annie to fully comprehend what happened to her that day. It wasn't just a physical event, but also emotional and spiritual as well. After awakening from the procedure, and laying on her gurney, she frantically called to the nurse telling her, "I've changed my mind: I don't want to have an abortion." The nurse tried to comfort her but it was too late. Annie felt completely overwhelmed by remorse. She turned on the gurney, vomited on the floor and let out a gut-wrenching cry. Her baby was lost forever. [207]

Filled With Grief and Starting Over

With nowhere to turn, broken hearted, empty and disillusioned, Annie called her brother, Don, who was living in Las Vegas.

Don came to his sister's assistance by opening his home to her. After Annie's recovery from the abortion, she considered going back to college at the nearby University of Nevada. One afternoon, Annie joined some friends who wanted to visit the school's student union. While waiting to hook up with her friends, Annie noticed a huge bulletin board near the entrance of the building with hundreds of posted announcements. One advertisement caught her eye: "Female singer wanted for rock band." Excitedly, she snatched the ad off the wall and made plans to audition with the band.

The well known Robert Morris Agency (RMA) represented the band, Cruiser. After auditioning, Meadows discovered that she had been selected as their vocalist. News of her selection put Annie back on top of the world again. Her successful audition was attended by the band's bassist Peter Tibone and Cruiser's four other musicians. Her selection signaled a brighter future. Within a month of moving to Las Vegas, Annie joined the band, Cruiser, and prepared to go on tour. She became good friends with Peter, who drove her regularly to the band's nightly practice sessions.

While once a Christian, Tibone had abandoned his beliefs. Although Peter's family had strong ties to traditional Christianity, he had walked away from his faith a few years before meeting their new female vocalist. Tibone, along with the other band members were primarily committed to becoming successful rock musicians.

Even with all the recent changes in her life, Annie continued to practice witchcraft. Her skill level in the craft had developed to the point where she could move small objects with her mind, a skill known as telekinesis. As a young girl, (before she left home), Annie had actually teleported herself from one place to another, on a couple of occasions. Her uncanny ability to predict the future, with the use of tarot cards, visions and fortune telling, continued to amaze friends and acquaintances.

Dating back to the Old Testament, witchcraft is "commonly defined as the use of supposed magical powers to influence people and events... It is also known as sorcery and has been the part of the folklore of many societies for centuries." [208] Peter was aware of his girlfriend's secret and even though he had dismissed the idea of Christianity, he knew that the Bible condemned witchcraft. He recognized that there was clearly something wrong with Annie's obsessive fascination with black magic, witchcraft and the occult.

Meadow's high level of skill in sorcery made her feel extraordinarily powerful. As she continued delving into the world of dark magic, she regularly made contact with spirits. She even had periodic specter of a strange man with a black hooded cloak who seemed to shadow her and haunt her with visions. The visions debilitated the young, aspiring vocalist.

That year Cruizer headed off to Hawaii to start their much awaited overseas tour. The RMA agency cooperated by agreeing to transport the band's equipment (including amplifiers, speakers, microphones, and music instruments) and pay for the band's accommodations for their tour. RMA saw to it that the band had a fairly rigorous schedule and would fulfill their contractual obligations to the agency.

A Life-Changing Moment

On a rare evening off, while staying in a condo on the island of Oahu, Annie received an unexpected call from her mother, Aileen. Aileen told her daughter of a conversation she had had at church with a long time family friend, Donna Thompson. Thompson told her friend that God had given her a word saying, "Annie will be a Gospel singer one day with a large ministry." Annie reacted angrily to her mother, shouting over the phone, "I will never sing gospel music and I will never sing in a church. I am going to be a rock star." [209]

After six months in the Hawaiian Islands, the strain of nonstop touring started to adversely affect the young vocalist. Meadows remembers one day, while she was in her accommodations in Kauai, looking straight at the ceiling and saying defiantly, "Okay, if there is a God out there – get me out of here, do something for me and get me out of this contract." [210]

The very next day, Annie was astonished to discover that the small island of Kauai was in the path of a devastating hurricane. Annie's band was staying in a guest house on Kauai at the time and it was one of the only houses in their neighborhood that was not severely damaged by the hurricane force winds. Within twenty four hours of Annie's defiant challenge to God, the storm had struck and passed.

Her band tried to recover their pieces of equipment, but just as the buildings around them, the damage was too great. Certainly the band couldn't play without their gear. When asked if the night club had insurance for the catastrophe, band members heard these words, "No, because the insurance company claimed it was an act of God." Almost immediately, Annie remembered back to the bizarre bargain she demanded of God. The storm made a clear impression on the young singer. [211]

Cruiser was forced to cut short its tour and head back home to Las Vegas. Once home, Annie found work at the Golden Nugget Casino, working the baccarat table.

Again, Annie was able to stay at her brother Don's house. Her co-worker at the Casino, Yona Montero, periodically made it a point to talk about God's love; often quoting passages about subjects from the Bible; but nothing she said really mattered to Annie. Annie wanted to live her own life and do her own thing as a witch. Even so, she still deeply cared for her friend, Peter. While on Kauai, Annie had begun to fall in love with Tibone. They had spent an inordinate amount of time together, and he had somehow made his way into her heart.

Moved by what happened in Kauai, Peter decided to turn back to his Christian roots. He repeatedly tried to share passages from his Bible with Annie but she would only listen passively. Despite his girl-friend's apathy, Peter started attending Calvary Chapel in Las Vegas. After many attempts to get Annie to visit church, she finally agreed.

Going to Church

She dressed for church as if she was going to a rock concert. Wearing a black witch outfit, Annie left for church that evening with Peter. During the service, Annie noticed that many of the people in the church seemed happy and appeared friendly to the young couple. However, Annie became jittery and uncomfortable when she heard the pastor's message. She asked Peter, "How long is this going to be?"[212] Annie stormed out of the church building that evening telling Peter, "I've had enough of this!"

Annie's experience with the church that evening convinced her that she really needed more fun. She saw herself as a sex, drugs, and rock & roll kind of girl. She wanted nothing to do with this old fashioned church stuff.

After Annie's scene at the church, Peter dropped her off at her brother's house and drove away. She stood in the front yard of her brother's house—all alone. Stars sparkled in the sky and the night appeared silent. All alone in the driveway, Annie shook her fist at the sky and screamed at God; a God she often said she did not believe in. She yelled out, "I hate you! You have taken my boyfriend and have messed with my parent's minds. This is MY life and I will live it as I see fit."[213]

Suddenly, Annie heard a small voice speak to her. She recognized the voice because she had heard the voice of God when she was a very little girl. The still small voice gently spoke to her saying, "You still have a choice, Annie. You can choose to walk away from me or come to me." That memorable evening ended with those precious words that she will never forget. [214]

A few days later Annie woke up to the sound of her clock radio. Yet, instead of hearing the usual alarm going off, Annie was slowly awakened by music. The first sounds she heard were from the popular singer, Amy Grant. The melody and lyrics of the song deeply touched Meadows. Years later Annie recalled the moment when she "was never so moved. Tears were streaming down my face ...." [215] She was deeply touched as she intently listened to the lyrics El Shaddai. As a trained singer she paid close attention to each word, each phrase of Grant's song. It was as if the lyrics and the melody of the song reached out and told her how much God really loved and cared just for her.

To this day, Annie doesn't have a clue how a religious song played on her radio. She questioned how any music even played that morning. Annie had set the alarm to go off by itself but not with the radio. It was also a mystery how the radio dial ended up on a Christian station. She could not find any explanation that made sense to her. Annie resolved to return to the church, for the Sunday evening service. Annie again dressed in her black witch cape, however deep in her heart she had an interest this time in hearing what the minister had to say. When the pastor asked if anyone wanted to start their lives over and wipe the slate clean, Annie reluctantly raised her hand. She still wondered, "What can Jesus do for me?" [216] Over time Annie found out. Her life has never been the same since that day. As a new Christian, friends prayed for her. She has felt the touch of a divine love that she had never experienced before. "Nothing would replace that moment," she proclaimed later.

Annie later admitted that her "conversion was a dramatic one but it was something that she would never regret, even for a minute." [217] Meadows decided to get rid of all of her witchcraft paraphernalia. She traveled with Peter to a near-by desert and burned every occult item she owned. Her tarot cards, witches cape, marijuana pipe, witch-craft books, black magic paraphernalia and other symbols from her former life were all destroyed that day.

Almost eighteen months later, Peter and Annie exchanged wedding vows before their friends and relatives. What a happy occasion for the young couple! Even with all the exciting new changes in her life, Annie still felt troubled at times by her dark past.

The dark image of the man with a black-hooded cape continued to haunt her. Occasionally, she even saw demons from the spirit worlds that were not of Jesus Christ. They caused fear to confuse Annie but she remembered Peter telling her about the power of the name of Jesus Christ. On those occasions, Peter urged Annie to invoke Christ's name. As Annie became more comfortable with using the name of Christ, the spiritual manifestations and demonic oppression began to disappear.

This spiritual tug of war lasted for a while. Annie became tired of these repetitive spiritual encounters. One day she asked God for help and He gave it to her. That still small voice encouraged her to read Psalm 91. The famous Psalm calmed her fears, but it took years before Meadows learned to fully let go of the fear. [218]

Annie's passion for singing gradually led her into a gospel singing career that earlier she had totally denied and rejected. With a humble yet memorable beginning, Annie accepted the position of worship leader in her church. She loved the camaraderie with the other worship team members. Her pastor encouraged her to reach out and use her God-given talents to sing.

Unknown to Annie, as the New Year's Eve service approached, her senior pastor had scheduled her to open for Darrell Mansfield, a recording artist for Maranatha Records. While initially reluctant to perform as a solo artist, Annie made the best of her thirty minute performance. On that night, she discovered just how much she enjoyed singing and sharing God's love through her music. God had given Annie the gift of song and music. She took that gift and now has shared it around the world through her ministry (Faithrunner Incorporated).

Annie released her very first recording, Courage, a mixture of rock and ballad music with positive feedback and acceptance. Since then, Annie has released five other CDs that follow music styles ranging from classical, and Celtic, to pop, jazz and Christmas themed tunes.

As a gospel singer, Annie has collaborated and worked with such notable Christian artists as Jars of Clay, White Heart, Sheila Walsh, Russ Taff, Bryan Duncan, Michael O'Brian, Darrell Mansfield, Rebecca St. James and David Meece. Besides traveling throughout the United States, Annie's ministry reaches a worldwide audience.[219]

Today, Annie continues to reach out to people through her concerts and appearances with the same message of love, hope and forgiveness that she found in the pages of the Bible. In Revelation 3:20, Jesus tells us, "Look! I have been standing at the door and I am constantly knocking. If anyone hears me calling him and opens the door, I will come in and fellowship with him and he with me" (Living Bible).

If you care to get in touch with Annie Meadows and learn more about her world-wide ministry, she can be reached through her website: www.Faithrunner.org

Clearly, Annie's story tells us all that no matter where you have been, God can take you somewhere better.

Chapter 10

Josh Hamilton A Texas Ranger Outfielder's Miracle from God

E very person alive has some kind of God given talent or skill; something that they can use to maximize their life. Sometimes, the revelation of how to do that is obvious, yet for others it can take years of fumbling around in the dark and lots of humiliating failures to reach their potential. Those who were close to Josh Hamilton knew that he was blessed with unmistakable talent early in life.

Even at a very young age, it became obvious that Josh was blessed with a raw athletic ability that surpassed that of his peers. Born on May 21, 1981, Hamilton joined the family as the youngest son of Tony and Linda Hamilton of Raleigh, North Carolina. Josh's older brother, Jason, also excelled in sports. The boys' parents became very supportive of both their sons' athletic endeavors during their early years. Jason acknowledged in a 2011 interview that he and his brother Josh had a great time growing up. [220]

Josh played a variety of competitive sports in school including track, baseball and football. His father, Tony, spent hours with his son in batting practice as well as coaching. Tim Stephens, a local sports reporter for the News & Observer remembered noticing that "behind the Hamilton's house, the T-ball, net and a back wall that were all well worn" from the many hours the youngster spent time there hitting baseballs.[221] It seemed all Josh ever wanted to do was play on and be around a team.[222]

Josh's brother Jason (born in 1977) graduated from Athens Drive High School in Raleigh, N.C. in 1995, the same year Josh started high school. Jason had already established himself as one of the school's statistical record holders in baseball. But Josh became determined to make his mark in sports there as well.[223] By the time Josh started high school Jason had gone on to attend college at the University of North Carolina for a year before enlisting in the U.S. Marine Corps, after which he married.

Josh played centerfield and also pitched for the Athens Drive Jaguars. His heroics in baseball gained him notoriety in the local newspaper. According to Devil Ray's Manager Chuck LaMar: Josh Hamilton "can run. He can field. He can throw. He can hit. And he can hit with power."[224] Tim Stephens, a Raleigh sports reporter, agreed after seeing Josh play many times as a high school baseball player. Interest grew in the young man's ability to where baseball scouts regularly watched Jaguar games.

Josh Hamilton's throwing speed off the mound clocked in excess of 95 mph by the time he started his senior year. His incredible strike out to pitch ratio (91 strike-outs in 56 innings) resulted in only one loss while on the mound during his final year with the Jaguars. The Athens Drive senior's batting stats were equally impressive (batting .529 with thirty RBIs and thirteen home runs) when opposing pitchers didn't intentionally walk him. Incredibly, he struck out only four times during his last year in high school baseball and had twenty stolen bases.[225] Scouts and fans alike marveled at the young player's fluid hitting swing. Many teams decided if they had a chance to draft the North Carolina native ball player, they'd select him as an everyday player (instead of a rotation pitcher).

News and Observer reporter, Tim Stephens, remembered one game when Josh hit a home run so quickly that the ball "left so fast, it took off like a line drive."[226] It wasn't unusual for scouts to describe Josh's playing ability as a "classic five-tool player.' Hamilton's draft prospects grew by leaps and bounds and earned him a feature story in Baseball America, a popular sports magazine for baseball enthusiasts.

Stephens also recalled when the future star went out of his way to befriend Ashley Pittman, the team's equipment manager (a special needs student). Josh's friendly relationship with Pittman said a lot about the young athlete's character. [227]

Hamilton's high school career ended on a high note in June of 1999. The Athens Drive player was selected as the # 1 choice in the MLB (Major League Baseball) draft. He also became the first high school outfielder to be drafted No. 1 since Ken Griffey in 1987. Josh joined the small, elite group of high school baseball players (like Chipper Jones, Ken Griffey and Alex Rodriguez) who were picked as No. 1 choices in the draft. [228]

Playing Professional Ball

Josh's parents, Linda and Tony, quit their jobs and went on the road with him as he began his professional career with stops in Princeton, W.Va., Fishkill, N.Y., and Charleston, S.C. "They followed behind the team bus in their truck and stayed at the same hotels.... Linda even cooked Josh's meals, and Tony broke down his son's performance after every game." [229]

Unaware of the danger that lay ahead, his mother was driving on February 28, 2001. With Josh and his father as passengers, a truck ran a red light and rammed them. Not only did the young baseball player suffer a back injury in the accident, but his mother sustained serious injuries as well. Tony accompanied his wife back to Raleigh (North Carolina) to receive much needed medical attention. [230]

For the first time in his life, Josh Hamilton found himself separated from the two people closest to him. Tampa Bay's management, along with their AA minor league affiliate, placed Josh on the injured reserve list once the baseball club realized the extent of the prized draft choice's injury.

For a number of months, Hamilton's forced inactivity gave the twenty-year old the kind of free time he hadn't really experienced before. Josh found himself hanging out at a tattoo parlor in Bradenton, Florida. Some of his new acquaintances did not have the same upbringing as Josh and he started making unwise decisions that ultimately cast a dark shadow over the next several years of his life. Thus began a struggle that was new for Josh—a battle with drug and alcohol addiction.

Over the course of the next four years, Josh roller coasted through a "pattern of rehabs and relapses, interspersed with short bursts of baseball until more injuries led to more free time, which led to more drugs, which eventually led to a suspension from baseball that grew by another twelve months with every failed test."[231] The saga continued for Josh, while his family and friends found it difficult to even discuss. Jason, later explained, "It hit our parents pretty hard, when they found out about Josh's chronic problems with alcohol and drugs."[232]

Like others from her community, Josh's grandmother Mary Holt had strong convictions of her faith in God. She trusted in Jesus Christ as her Lord and Savior with her whole heart. She believed in a God who listened to and answered the prayers of His children. Throughout the ages, God frequently has used friends, relatives and acquaintances to reach folks who are struggling with problems. Such was the case with Josh Hamilton. His substance abuse tormented those who truly loved him. Providentially, God used Josh's grandmother to reach out to her struggling grandson.

In October, 2005, Josh Hamilton found himself at his grandmother's door at 2:00 a.m. Mary "trudged to the door, looking through the peephole and saw a stranger on her porch ... It was as if she saw a ghost. Her grandson had lost 40 pounds. He hadn't slept in four days. His face was ashen. His cheeks were sunken. His eyes were glazed and distant. His body was trembling."[233] By the time Josh showed up at her door, he was a broken man. (Jason always knew that the one the person who would get through to Josh would be Mary, their grandmother.)[234] During the night Josh had a bad dream where he wrestled with the Devil. He would soon be ready to give his heart to the Prince of Peace, Jesus Christ.[235]

Still, it took another year for Josh to fully overcome the bad habits learned from his days at the Tattoo Parlor. "Addiction to drugs or alcohol wasn't something what the Lord wanted for him," his grandmother would say. Jason said his brother knew that after his talk with Mary that if he was to commit his life to God, he also needed to fully commit himself to being fully restored. [236]

The Journey toward Restoration

Josh Hamilton had heard the story of the prodigal son. He had spent long hours talking to another mentor, Michael "Big Daddy" Chadwick, who was to be his future father-in-law. Chadwick had talked to Josh about the value of making wise choices. Chadwick instructed the former MLB draft choice, "There is no middle ground... You either die or you get well." Ultimately, Chadwick knew, "The only way to get him back was to love him back." [237]

Chadwick knew the Christian message of redemption and forgiveness was the most important message that Josh Hamilton could hear.

Another person who had a powerful impact on Josh's life was his girlfriend, Katie Chadwick. Almost a year from the time he knocked on his grandmother's door, Josh and Katie were married. Yet within a relatively short period of time, Josh fell into another addictive relapse. This occurrence broke the heart of Josh's young wife. Katie discovered that she needed to forgive him since her bitterness caused her intense pain. As a deeply religious person and in an effort to please God, Katie learned to forgive her husband for his misdeeds. She also learned that she could not change him. Only Josh could do that—if he wanted to. She did, however, change her attitude about him and over time, her husband improved. [238]

News of Josh's commitment to God and his desire to break away from a life of substance abuse appeared in an article in the St. Petersburg Times. Roy Silver, Vice President of local Clearwater baseball academy, The Winning Inning, read a copy of the newspaper article. As Silver read the story about Hamilton's off-field struggles, he felt a small tug in this heart. Somehow Silver knew that God wanted him to reach out to the young man.

Roy Silver had an extensive background in professional sports and had been with the St. Louis Cardinal Baseball organization as both a player and coach (1984-1997). From 1997 to 1999 he was an

'A' league manager for the Tampa Bay baseball club, the same organization that originally drafted Josh Hamilton in 1999.

Silver's Winning Inning Academy operated out of the Jack Russell Memorial Stadium in Clearwater, Florida. The stadium, built in 1955, once had been the spring training facility for the National League's Philadelphia Phillies baseball club. In his work with the academy, Silver shared his primary focus on "developing quality baseball players from the inside out." Silver applied his strong foundation in Christ which models how he teaches and interacts with his players at the Winning Inning Academy. [239]

In 2006, Roy invited Josh to be a contributing part of the academy. Hamilton soon accepted Silver's invitation. According to Silver, the former Tampa Bay draft choice "got to experience the whole process (of our academy) as he stayed there for four months." Roy felt Josh's experience at the academy would help him prepare for life. Silver's goal for each participant of his program is "to develop the whole person: mind, soul and body." Roy later acknowledged, "To Josh's credit, he was thirsty for the Word of God." [240]

In his stay at the academy, Hamilton "got up at 7:30 a.m. every morning, ate breakfast and worked. He mowed the outfield and watered the infield. (He) pulled weeds and cleaned toilets ... and in his spare time he honed the skills that once had scouts comparing him to Mickey Mantle." [241]

Over time Josh performed most of the jobs (i.e. ground keepers, custodians, handy men, and instructors) of those who were a part of the baseball operation. Roy believed that Josh needed to earn his keep. His experience at the academy helped him learn to appreciate everything behind a successful small business like The Winning Inning academy. [242]

During this time, God clearly had his hand on Josh's gradual yet miraculous transformation out from under the substance abuse. Katie realized that God intended to give her husband back to her. She also saw the joy Josh got from playing baseball. [243]

In less than nine months the MLB reinstated Josh Hamilton. The league became convinced that the former first round draft choice deserved another chance despite his long hiatus from professional baseball. Three years after his first drug suspension, Josh Hamilton took to the field for the Devil Ray's affiliate team at Hudson Valley. It was a cherished moment for the North Carolina native.

Despite the fact that the Tampa Bay baseball club had invested millions in the twenty-five-year-old player, the team's management decided to exclude Josh from their forty man roster. With this decision, Hamilton became eligible for the annual Rule 5 draft –open to players who were available for free-agency from their previous signed teams.

On December 6th, Josh learned of his draft to the Chicago Cubs only to be traded to the Cincinnati Reds the same day. Cincinnati Reds Manager and North Carolina native, Jerry Narron, was keenly aware of Josh's athletic abilities. Upon hearing of the outcome of the draft, Jerry told the Washington Post, "I was so excited knowing his history and knowing him personally." [244]

Narron's brother, Johnny, also had a deep love for baseball. As one of Josh's coaches when he played baseball as a youngster, Johnny reacquainted himself with the legendary slugger. The Narron family had deep roots in baseball and even their uncle played for the St. Louis Cardinals in the 1943 World Series.

The Cincinnati head coach eventually assigned his brother the duty of being the club's "major league video and administrative coach... (However) Johnny's first order of business was Hamilton: making sure the former Athens Drive star was staying on the path to recovery." Johnny accompanied Hamilton on the road, "where they stayed in adjoining rooms. They dined together. They prayed together, too." [245]

On the Field Again

By the end of the 2007 season, Josh ended up playing in ninety games and had a solid year at the plate. The North Carolina native had a .292 batting average, a .368 on base average and hit nineteen home runs that year for the Reds. Nevertheless, Hamilton became expendable because the Cincinnati team needed pitching. The team already had several quality outfielders (Ken Griffey and Adam Dunn to name a few) so a trade made sense to the Cincinnati club.[246]

The American League's Texas Rangers showed genuine interest in acquiring the former #1 MLB draft choice. The baseball club needed to fill a hole they had in their outfield as well as obtaining another strong hitter to compliment some of the talent the team already possessed. The Rangers were willing to part with two of their strong pitching prospects, Danny Herrera and Edinson Volquez for the Cincinnati outfielder. So the trade took place.

After three seasons it appeared that both teams had benefited from this baseball transaction. Herrera had been designated the starting pitcher and leader of the Red's pitching rotation for their 2011 season. As for Josh, he had three solid seasons with the Rangers in '08 and '09, batting .304 and .268 respectively.[247]

As for 2010, Josh capped off a stellar pennant winning season for the Rangers, by batting .359 with thirty-two home runs and 100 RBIs. After realizing (near the close of the final AL championship game) that his team was going to reach the World Series for the first time, Hamilton told a Boston Herald report, "I was thinking about where I was, and everything I went through and how God was just faithful ... to bring me out of the dark part of my life."[248]

Even though he felt disappointment that his team didn't win the World Series in 2010 against the National League Champion Giants, Josh Hamilton saw his team as having a break out year. The Rangers won their first division title in eleven years and made their first World Series appearance in club history.

In public appearances, the Texas Ranger's star acknowledged winning in 2010 and receiving the American League's Most Valuable Player title as a humbling experience. In January (2011) Josh accepted the award given by the Baseball Writers Association. In response to this great honor, Josh told them all, "I want to thank Jesus Christ because without Him I would not be here." In a touching moment, he continued his speech by saying that he that he wanted to also thank his wife.

Josh's father-in-law, Michael Chadwick, understood the significance of that moment. He understood the miraculous journey his son-in-law had traveled. As part of the audience that day, Chadwick just wanted to stand on his seat and declare to the world that "standing before you is a miracle of God." He felt a similar pride for his daughter, Katie and quickly acknowledged, "She taught me so much about trusting God." Chadwick's love and affection for his daughter and son-in-law only goes to show how important family is to the Hamilton clan. Like Josh, Michael's faith in God continues to be the most important part of his life. [249]

Living Victoriously

More than ever Josh Hamilton remains aware of his close call with being just another statistic in the destructive culture of drug and alcohol dependency that so tragically plagues millions of lives around the country. He is forever thankful for the second chance God has given him to live his new life in Christ.

Today, Josh and Katie Hamilton are using their platform and notoriety to reach out to the public with the message of love and hope that is so graciously conveyed by their Lord and Savior, Jesus Christ. Several years ago, the couple founded Triple Play Ministries. [250] The ministry has become a conduit for the dozens of off season appearances they make and also organizes Christian baseball camps and supports orphanage work as well.

Josh and Katie Hamilton see themselves as a team. They have discovered that nothing much of any importance is accomplished through purely human strength. It's clear to see that life takes team-work and through its ups and downs the #1 pick for your team needs to be Jesus Christ.

Chapter 11

Michael Glatze Young Gay America's Managing Editor Finds Truth

L ife can have many unexpected turns. It is simply a given that everyone experiences but how we handle those changes either turns life into an adventure or a nightmare. Michael still remembers the good times spent in the safety of his tree house at his picturesque Olympia, WA home. He remembers looking out into a neighboring forest with its wandering running trails. Those were the days of innocence that gave no warning of the tough times that lay ahead.

Carl and Cathy Elliott Glatze welcomed their son, Michael, into the world on January 27, 1975 with great joy and excitement. For the first three years of Michael's life, the Glatze family lived in nearby Tacoma and then moved to Olympia, Washington where Michael spent a memorable early childhood.

When Michael was just nine years old, Cathy discovered that her husband was having an affair and decided to file for divorce. The impending divorce that loomed on the horizon had a profound effect on Michael. He remembers most about those anxious days, "The feeling of fear and the hurt (he) felt when he found out that his parents were getting a divorce." [251]

To support her son and six-year-old daughter, Cathy found work at a local sporting goods store. Her income supplemented the child support and, with the stipend money she earned from writing a sport running column in the local newspaper still barely covered the essentials. The divorce was finalized in 1984.

Michael recalls knowing what the word 'divorce' meant but lacked the coping skills he needed to handle the stress. He remembers being sorely afraid and "deeply affected by the pain I knew his mother was experiencing." Still, the young teenager could not fully comprehend the depth of that hurt. He reacted by trying to protect her. He shared, "I became resentful towards my father...even angry at him." He also spoke openly as an adult saying, "At an early age, I also was confused about who I was and how I felt about others."[252] Betrayal is the word that came to Michael's mind when he thought of his father.

Michael sought to find ways of protect and defend his mother and sister, but due to the family's deteriorating financial condition, Michael, Cathy and Laura had to move. They could only afford a small, meager home in the low income section of Tumwater.

Even though Michael still harbored a deep-seated hostility towards his father Carl, he wisely decided it would be more constructive to vent his energy by excelling in school. Academically he rose to the top but socially, he remained isolated. He felt 'different' and stuffed his emotions deep inside, never talking to anyone. Michael shared, "Sometimes I would pray to Jesus as a kid." His relatives including his grandmother, Elizabeth Elliott, Malia (Cathy's sister) and Koa Siu (his cousin) were all Bible-believing Christians and that certainly helped.

Excelling at School

At thirteen, his father died of a heart defect. He attended his father's funeral but a strong sense of betrayal and anger surfaced during the eulogy. Regardless of the emotions that raged through him, this teenager was determined to make his mark in life and it became important than ever for him to be there for his mom.

Michael continued to do well in school, and by his senior year he rose to the top of his class and was also named captain of both the track and cross country teams at school. During his four years at Tumwater, Glatze regularly surrounded himself with Christian and conservative friends. Perhaps because of, his academic achievements, Glatze considered himself to be a nerd. He did not see in himself what others recognized, as in his senior year he was elected president of Tumwater High's student body. [253]

Michael's academic pursuit during his high school years paid off. At year's end, he had the school's top GPA (grade point average). Upon news of his mother's diagnosis with stage four cancer, his sheer persistence enabled him to complete his last year of high school despite his heartache. He felt unbelievable pressure during that senior year.

He had an academic record that turned the heads of the college admissions boards. He finally decided he would apply to Dartmouth College, an ivy league school in the northeast. The school awarded Michael with an academic scholarship. Dartmouth offered "a superb undergraduate residential college with the intellectual character of a university, featuring thriving research and first-rate graduate and professional programs." [254]

Glatze walked onto Dartmouth campus in 1993. The Tumwater graduate commented, "I could see a new world in my future." The future appeared to be very promising. During this time his mother's health completely deteriorated. Overwhelmed with grief over her death in September of 1994, the bottom fell out of his world for he had lost the one person who loved him unconditionally.

In his own words, Michael became "very bitter," even to the point where he overtly "became angry at God when his mother died". Michael was still resentful over the divorce as he met with other family members at his mother's aunt home in Lincoln City, Oregon during his mother's funeral. Later, Michael traveled with his sister Laura to Mt. Rainer National Park to spread his mom's ashes around the base of a small fir tree overlooking a mountain lake.

Living a Gay Lifestyle

Michael returned to New Hampshire to make his mark at the ivy league college in 1994. At Dartmouth, Michael later stated that he 'felt superior' to his peers and believed himself to be on the cusp of accomplishing great personal achievements. Life as a student within

Dartmouth's 'enlightened' culture and dormitory life brought new feelings he had never before experienced.

Glatze also started having a "real desire to have a connection with (his) own masculinity." Since his father's death six years earlier, Michael had been afraid of dealing with his masculinity and "had closed himself off from his own sense of connection." [255] Looking back, he noticed that even in his mid-teens, he had been attracted to guys. At Dartmouth, he began to form a relationship with other males who "opened a whole new world to me." A gay professor at the college became the 'father figure' he had never had as a young boy.

Over the next six months at Dartmouth, Glatze became even more involved with the gay lifestyle. Keenly aware of and interested in learning about the history of the homosexual political movement through his friendship with his gay professor /advisor, he jumped in with both feet. Along with working hard on his English major, Glatze decided in his junior year to join the gay student alliance: DRA (the Dartmouth Rainbow Alliance).

Michael spent the summer before his senior year in San Francisco, working as an intern with the advocacy group called Stop Aids Project (SAP). The group, based in San Francisco, used various means and methods to communicate its directive and purpose of its organization. It was there that Michael met his future gay partner, Ben, who was originally from Nova Scotia.

During August of that summer Michael and other SAP volunteers traveled to San Diego, California where the (1996) Republican National Convention was being held. Glatze, along with more than one hundred other homosexual rights activists, were determined to present their aids awareness agenda to the media and the hundreds of conventions attendees.

Gathering close to a block from the Convention Center located near San Diego Bay, the SAP activists and other protestors caused quite a stir. Michael and his activist friends were determined to get their pro-gay message out to the public. On one particular day, Michael and his friends were protesting a Faith and Freedom event in Balboa Park. [256] A small group of elderly Christian ladies began praying for the activists. Instead of ignoring the group, Michael and his friends surrounded them, taunting them with crude epitaphs. Their efforts to intimidate the praying women didn't work. Instead one lady looked Michael right in the eyes and said, "I love you … and God loves you."[257]

Michael responded by yelling, "How dare you say that to me!" As he looked sternly into the eyes of this woman, she responded by saying, "It is my duty to love you." Within that brief moment, Michael felt a kind of sincerity and warmth he had never before experienced. Once back in San Francisco, Michael still felt that his participation in the gay rights movement "gave him a new sense of purpose." By summer's end in 1996, Michael returned to the northeast to finish his senior year while Ben temporarily moved back to Nova Scotia. Glatze was named leader of Dartmouth's Rainbow Alliance.

Graduating and Starting a Magazine

Michael proudly graduated from Dartmouth, after which he and Ben returned to the Mission District of San Francisco with aspirations of making their mark in the gay community. Ben worked as an architect in the city. Michael wrote an essay on 'Queer Theory' and was later hired as the Assistant Editor of XY Magazine.

XY Magazine hit the newsstands in 1996 as an appeal to gay youth. XY was founded by entrepreneur, Peter Ian Cummings, with the objective of teaching 'gay pride'. The staff of the magazine viewed the publication as a survival guide for young homosexual men and women.

Glatze made an impression and Cummings promoted him to the position of a XY magazine editor. While XY did have some "soft pornographic content," as Glatze would later say, the publication became a voice for homosexual causes and was instrumental in promoting gay political aspirations. As an editor of the publication, Glatze somewhat agreed with what GLSEN (Gay, Lesbian, Straight Education Network) founder and executive Kevin Jennings had been sharing. Both believed that gays needed "to queer the schools and get rid of any notion that heterosexuality is normal."[258] "While Jennings promoted tolerance towards homosexuals, he was unwilling to reciprocate by extending tolerance to those who disagreed with him." [259] Eight years later, Kevin Jennings was to be appointed by the Obama administration as the 'Safe Schools' Director for the U.S. Department of Education.

Michael and many of his gay friends remained "open to the possibility that everyone could become gay." [260] Under Cummings' leadership and with Michael's support (from 1999 to 2000) the magazine saw the subscriber base surge. Subscriptions to public libraries, schools, colleges, and young adults took off. Glatze became more determined than ever "to queer the schools." Michael and Ben even attempted to buy the magazine from Cummings but their effort failed. By May of 2001, Glatze decided to end his association with the magazine. It was time for him to expand his horizons, and so he and Ben traveled to Nova Scotia, where they lived for a while before moving to Boston.

The pair created a new web publication named, YGA (Young Gay America). Michael's commitment to his identity caused him to become as dedicated as ever to the gay lifestyle. Michael believed that he understood the predicament facing many youths in the gay community. Determined to express the stories of these young homosexuals, he and Ben set out to travel around the country to document stories of America's gay youth.

Michael Glatze wanted to be the voice for the voiceless. Interested in recruiting and building a movement of young gay people, Michael focused on educating the whole person about the homosexual community and their valiant cause. [261]

Michael and Ben acquired grant funding for YGA and they were hired to do a documentary film by Equality Forum on gay teen suicide. Equality Forum was founded by Malcom Lazin whose organization also promoted GLBT History Month. They also sponsored events involved with "the largest annual national and international GLBT civil rights forum." [262] (The group continues to be involved in providing support for gay friendly candidates and causes).

By 2004, the popularity of YGA started to burgeon. Glatze worked on extending the visibility of the magazine from web format to a print publication and also sought grants from various gay groups from around the country. During that year, a wealthy New England donor expressed interest in providing funding for the format change. To Michael and Ben, the offer was the fulfillment of a longtime dream.

Life appeared good for Glatze, who used his wide range of contacts to expand the distribution of the new print magazine. The attention he received from the cutting-edge magazine had a part in contributing to its success. In 2005 Michael was invited to be a panelist at the JFK Jr. Forum at Harvard's Kennedy School of Business. During this event, Michael began to harbor serious doubts about the direction his life was taking. He appeared to have it all...or did he?

Anxiety and Panic Lead to a Radical Change

Anxiety and panic attacks started creating obstacles in his life. As Michael's doubts mounted, his health took a nose dive. The stress of work and new evidence of severe stomach cramps in his body were cause for concern. Physically, Michael believed something was gravely wrong. He reflected back on his own father's heart failure and became more anxious.

Michael was not only dealing with questions about his own mortality but "colleagues (from work) began to notice he was going through some kind of a religious experience." [263] The young editor began voicing a profound fear of death. [264] His condition worsened to the point where he sought medical attention, including an electrocardiogram. He undertook another kind of examination as well. Turning to God, he asked some questions about life. Through this time of reflection, he discovered a deeper problem than his physical health. Michael admitted, "It hit me with total clarity that God was real."

Compulsion drove Michael to get a Bible. He went to a small bookstore and picked up a used copy. Michael remembers opening it to Matthew 5, where he read about the Sermon on the Mount. Glatze absorbed every single word. While he had once proclaimed, "This book is for bigots," the gay activist read with different eyes and felt inspired by the passages. Michael was overwhelmed by the "intelligent and insightful words of the young prophet from Nazareth." The unique spiritual insight of the thirty year old Jewish teacher amazed him. Inspired by the clarity of Christ's sermon, Michael decided to read through the rest of the New Testament.[265]

Glatze convinced himself that he could be both religious and an advocate for the gay lifestyle. He felt he had a "more enlightened version of Christianity ... thinking that 'I had God on my side.'" During the next few months, Michael delved into God's Word and became even more serious about his prayer life.

Several years later Glatze wrote in an article for World Net Daily, "After viewing my words on videotape of that (Kennedy School of Government) performance, I began to seriously doubt what I was doing in my life." For the next year and a half, Michael developed a blossoming relationship with God. Michael opened up to the reality that "there was a real me"—a real person who was created to have a close personal relationship with His Creator.

For much of the following year (2006) Michael continued on through a healing process; attempting to reconcile his lifestyle with his new found relationship with God. Passages like those he found in Romans 1:27 confirmed astonishing truths to him. Michael discovered that there are many scripture verses that speak to the whole man. By reading the Bible, Michael gained a whole new outlook on life. His opinions and perspectives were turning his life upside down.

For Michael Glatze, his most memorable day came when he decided to leave YGA magazine. Michael vividly recalls typing on his computer screen, "Homosexuality is death, and I choose life." Michael later admitted, "Healing from the wounds caused by homosexuality was not easy." But "coming out from under the influence of the homosexual mindset was the most liberating, beautiful and astonishing thing he ever experienced in his entire life."

Currently, Michael Glatze is attending Bible school with the intention of serving in full-time ministry. He already has served as a Chaplain for a ministry in Colorado, and written some intriguing commentaries for internet news group such as World Net Daily. Michael's favorite Bible verse speaks volumes about his courageous journey from his biological birth to his second birth into the family of God. "No temptation has overtaken you except what is common to mankind. And God is faithful; he will not let you be tempted beyond what you can bear. But when you are tempted, he will also provide a way out so that you can endure it." [266]

Today, there is peace in Michael's life. The transformation he has experienced has not happened overnight and it still continues to this day. Yet Michael understands just how unfathomable are the depths of God's love for him and each one of us. He knows that the God he serves is patient in our ever day journey through life. It leads each one of us to thoughtfully ask ourselves: how patient and persistent are we in developing our own relationship with God? For this question, each one of us needs to search sincerely in our hearts for the answer.

Chapter 12

Darren Carrington An NFL Veteran Discovers the Best Game Plan

D arren Carrington's football career was impressive. He played
in the National Football League for eight years on teams
including the Denver Broncos, the Detroit Lions, San Diego Chargers,
Jacksonville Jaguars and the Oakland Raiders. He made it to the
Super Bowl; not once but twice. However, to truly appreciate his
accomplishments you have to take the full journey back to where
his story first began.

Darren Russell Carrington was born on October 10, 1966 in
Jacobi Hospital in New York City. The one fan that cheered Darren
that day was his unwed mother, Beverly Carrington. Nicknamed
Buffy by his aunt, (for his strong, stout build), Darren spent his early
years in New York's Bronx River project. The project is a large public
housing complex that consisted of a number of clustered high rise
apartments. Each apartment cluster was made up of a fourteen story
apartment building that housed ten apartments on each floor.

To most outsiders, the projects and their surrounding neighborhood environment was intimidating, especially for someone
coming from a middle class suburban environment. The families
who lived there during Darren's early years watched out for each
other. Neighborhood gangs during those days consisted of friends

who hung out or usually associated with each other by age or ethnicity. Their friendships were helpful in providing a form of protection from any unwelcome intruders from outside the project.[268]

Darren's biological father chose not to be a part of his life
so Beverly sought help from her father, Frederick (a.k.a. Buddy)
Carrington. The family shared the three bedroom apartment in the
Bronx neighborhood, which enabled Darren to form relationships
with his uncle and two aunts. Buddy supported the family with his
job as a maintenance crew worker for a nearby apartment complex.

Beverly started working for Hertz rent-a-car as an accounts receiv-
able clerk when Darren was eight years old. He eventually got used to
coming home to an empty house and later referred to himself as the
latch key kid. Nevertheless, the young boy soon found other outlets
to occupy his time after school at the neighborhood sports complex.
Typically each NYC housing complex provided their community
with a sports and gym facility that served the needs of many of the
kids. One evening while watching ABC's Monday Night Football,
Darren turned to his mom and told her "Someday you will see me
playing football on television." Those words marked the beginning
of Carrington's lifelong dream of playing professional sports.[269]

One day when Buffy was ten, he was introduced to two young
men, Al Lewis and Carlos Perkins, the coaches at the project's local
community center. The facility they managed provided indoor basketball and other sports for latch key kids in their neighborhood.
Darren signed up and the fun began! These men dramatically influenced his life through their positive mentoring through sports.

After fighting with the unofficial school bully, Melvin, Darren was
given the choice of either going to another class at school CS-77, or
transfer to community school CS-102 so he chose to leave. Adjusting
to the new school was a challenge to the ten-year old boy. Once he
arrived at CS-102, Darren discovered what racial prejudice really
felt like. He didn't much like it. Fortunately for Darren, he recognized some other kids from his old neighborhood, and survived the
switch. By sixth grade Buffy was totally immersed in Pop Warner
football. Carrington's speed and agility gave him an edge as the

team's running back. He also enjoyed playing centerfield for the local baseball team each spring.

At twelve, Darren branched out into other sports. In track, he won the boy's fifty-yard dash and long jump championship in a city wide tournament. He also learned that he had to stay focused and stay out of trouble in order to succeed in football. [270]

Darren continued to play Pop Warner football through the eighth grade. His two coaches, Al Lewis and Carlos Perkins continued to provide a strong, positive influence in his life. Both men taught him personal discipline, respect and the importance of not swearing.

Darren welcomed his younger brother, Tajada, into the world in October 1980. Months earlier, Darren had been 'horsing around' with his friend, Bryant and Bryant's uncle: Frank Denson. Darren had expressed concern to his mother that Frank had played a little too rough with him after school. Beverly and Frank met to discuss his rough play with her son and over time, the two adults became romantically involved. Ultimately, Frank became the father that Darren had never had; the one who instilled discipline, perseverance and offered him encouragement.

As Darren approached his high school years, the Carrington family had to make an important choice. Which school should Darren attend? Ultimately, Carrington decided to go to DeWitt Clinton School primarily because DeWitt's football team had a stellar reputation. Established in 1897, DeWitt Clinton started out as an all-boy's public school. The school had an impressive list of former graduates including writer James Baldwin, actor Burt Lancaster, playwright Neil Simon, designer Ralph Lauren, NBA Hall of Fame member Nate Archibald, A&M records co-founder Jerry Moss and many others. [271]

Prior to entering his first year Darren tried out for the school's football team. Darren realized he would be practicing against some extremely talented defensive players. At only 5'6" and weighing around 150 lbs., Carrington felt small but he had confidence in his God-given talent. The coaches took one look at Darren's size and really never gave him a legitimate chance to compete for a roster spot on the team.

This rejection and disappointment affected Darren's attitude and his grades correspondingly fell as well. Darren still hoped that one day his dream would come true despite the recent setback. He planned to attend another school the coming year where he might have a better chance at playing football. While he waited, he placed his hopes and dreams in playing professional sports above things like "getting in trouble with girls or dabbling with marijuana". Darren admitted "doing those things were not going to help me get to where I'm going." He became even more determined to do what he needed to succeed.[272]

Other motivating factors would have a lasting impression on the teenager as well. Beverly's son remembered seeing his 19 year old cousin being sentenced to jail for armed robbery. He also recalled how alcohol abuse had such a detrimental effect on his biological father. It became obvious to Darren that sports were a way to get out of the projects.[273] Darren was already aware that he would have to make sacrifices to obtain his goals as he recognized the sacrifices his mother had made for him. Even if he didn't like some aspects of school, he vowed to make the best of his circumstances. Quitting was not in his vocabulary!

When the school year ended in late May, Darren enrolled in summer school. He decided to work within the system, and took the necessary steps needed to get another chance to try out for the team. Deep down inside he knew, he had to get through high school in order to obtain his dream.[274] That next fall, he enrolled in James Monroe High School which he once vowed he'd never attend, due to its poor football program. Entering as a junior, Darren was determined to make the best of this new opportunity.

Monroe's varsity football team had only two football coaches and no rich football tradition in those days. To be honest, the football team didn't even have its own locker room. Darren remembered his stepfather taping him up prior to games on his living room couch. Darren played defense (safety and rover). There were noticeable improvements in the defense during this first year.[275]

By his senior year, Darren weighed in at 175 pounds and stood 5'11". He finally played on the offensive team as wing back, running back and wide receiver. Darren started a terrific season until he suffered a severe hip injury which derailed him and kept him from playing out the entire season. Still, the high school senior believed himself destined to play college football.

At the end of his senior year, Darren made the decision to attend the University of Pittsburgh (UP). He successfully improved his grades in school and received his acceptance letter to the university. As a freshman, Carrington showed determination by trying to make the university's football team as a walk on player. He thought it an honor to play on the same team for which the former Dallas Cowboy running back, Tony Dorsett, had once played.

He did not make the team but he did not let go of his dream. With sheer determination, he played intramural football to keep in shape — physically and emotionally. He rallied more than ever to find a school that would give him a football scholarship. Darren decided to write to twenty-five different colleges, asking them for a chance to make their college football team.

Playing College Football

Only two colleges responded to Darren's inquiries, Northern Arizona University (NAU) and Mississippi Valley State. Carrington decided to enroll at NAU "on a hope and a prayer." [276] Once he arrived on campus, it was humbling to find out that he wasn't as quick and fast as he once thought he was. Darren's hope for a scholarship that year quickly faded.

As an NCAA transfer student, Darren had to red-shirt his first incoming year at the college. Nevertheless, he believed if the school would give him a scholarship – it would all be worth it. Darren had to work his way through school that first year just to pay tuition. He had to prove himself at every turn!

He met with the head coach and explained that he would not be returning without some kind of football scholarship. Inquiring about which positions were available for a scholarship, his coach's response was defensive back. Darren decided to take this new chal-lenge and become the best defensive back he could be.

When the '87 fall football campaign started, NAU coaches offered Darren a partial football scholarship to attend the school. His coaches thought he'd be best utilized by playing defense and special teams. During the fourth game, Coach Paul Arslanian asked Carrington to start as defensive cornerback. In his first starting game as a cornerback, Darren picked off two interceptions against Eastern Washington University, in a 34-24 win. Darren's athleticism and his play-making ability convinced the coaching staff that the young athlete should be upgraded to a full scholarship.

Darren returned to the Bronx that summer a happy man. Not only was he close to being the first member of his family to graduate from college, he had caught a glimpse of success. Back home that summer, Darren worked as a messenger clerk for a NY law firm. He also spent a lot of time in the gym getting ready for the upcoming football season. All the sacrifices, extra work and long hours were finally paying off.[277]

With enthusiasm Darren arrived back at the University's football camp in great condition. He already had a productive pre-season camp. His team even practiced near the field where the NFL Arizona Cardinals met. Darren remembered one of his coaches hinting that a professional career was not out of reach for the young NAU defensive back. Such encouragement made Darren realize just how far he had come. Darren was determined, more than ever, to make the best of this opportunity.

Darren Carrington now measured in at 6'2" tall and weighed between 185-190 pounds at the onset of his senior year in college and was considered a big defensive back. He now felt he had the physical skills to compete at the professional level.

Starting as one of the team's two defensive cornerbacks, his greatest thrill that season was running back a 99 yard kick-off return for a touchdown. His overall performance earned him an invitation to participate in the National Football League's combine game held in February (1989) for incoming professional football prospects.[278]

Reaching the Pro Ranks

Darren fondly remembered his senior year at NAU, watching the Arizona Cardinal's football team practice for the first time at their Flagstaff football facility. On a Friday in February of 1989, Darren traveled to Indianapolis, Indiana to attend the National Football League (NFL) combine. Darren was overwhelmed by emotion, but above all, had confident enthusiasm and anticipation as he realized his life-long dream was at last going to be realized.

That Saturday morning, the scouts timed each of the defensive backs and measured their speed, agility, athletic performance, and football related drills. Defensive backs from colleges all over the country underwent a thorough physical exam. Darren's time in the forty-yard dash was 4.5 seconds—his best time to this very day! [279]

As his senior year wound down, Darren felt proud to be the first person in his family to graduate from college. Up to this point, Darren had faced much adversity but his life long goal of becoming a professional athlete seemed to be in reach.

Even with less than twenty-four hours before the weekend draft (during April of '89), the NAU athlete spent part of the day working out for other NFL clubs. This time, it was the New York Giants. Such last minute assessments were common practice for pro-scouts during this most important time period for college football prospects. With hours before the weekend draft, emotions were running high for Darren, his family and friends.

The NAU senior was anxious to hear from any NFL team that wanted the all-league player. Darren's girlfriend, Vickie, was there for him every step of the way. On that Saturday in April, friends gathered in his NAU dormitory room to see the national telecast of the NFL draft. Late that Saturday when the draft had entered its third round, the twenty-two-year old senior decided to take off on his bike and ride around the school campus. The selection process and the pressure of the draft itself got to him. Not far into his ride, he began hearing cries and screams from friends who were trying to flag him down. He distinctly remembered hearing some girls yelling and shouting, "Denver's on the phone ... Denver's on the phone... They want to talk to you!" [280]

With wild excitement, Darren rushed back to his dorm room. As he reached for the phone, his heart pounded. Denver Bronco's Head Coach, Dan Reeves, was on the line ... waiting to talk to the man of the hour. While both Reeves and Carrington had a relatively short conversation that day, Denver's newest NFL draft pick was elated! The Bronco's Head Coach congratulated the NAU student on being selected in the fifth round, the 134th pick overall. [281] Within weeks, Carrington flew to meet his future employer. His life long dream was unfolding before his eyes.

The Denver Broncos were a thriving American Football Conference franchise in the late '80s. As one of eight original AFL franchises, Darren knew he had to work hard just to make the team. In both 1987 and 1988 Coach Dan Reeves had coached teams that were to become champions of the American Football Conference and had led the team to the Super Bowl. Darren knew he would have to produce.

Carrington was excited when he arrived at the rookie training camp in July of '89. With the help of his agent, Frank Murtha, he secured a two-year contract with the Broncos. The rookie needed a solid training camp to impress his new coaches. Veteran Steve Sewell befriended Darren and invited him to a midweek chapel service attended by other Denver teammates. He accepted and heard about God's love and forgiveness that night.

Darren realized that he had tried to be a success on his own and welcomed the idea of leaning on a higher power. However shallow Darren's past spiritual experience might have been, the NFL rookie wanted to personally meet the God the minister described that night. He wanted peace in his life and longed for some reliable direction.

Darren and Vickie also called upon Almighty God for help on December 31, 1989 when their one-pound-five-ounce miracle baby was born. They named her Diarra. With their daughter's premature birth and Vickie's schooling at NAU, the couple decided that Vickie and Diarra should remain in Arizona. God heard their prayers and their tiny baby began to thrive.

Carrington's Denver team appeared in the 1990 Super Bowl. While his team experienced a humiliating defeat that day, Carrington's thirty-nine-yard kickoff return set up the Bronco's only touchdown score. Darren's total of 146 yards in kickoff returns (averaging 24.3 yards per carry) still ranks fourth all-time in Super Bowl games.

The day before the first game of the second season, Darren was notified by Denver that they did not plan to renew his contract. Apparently, the Colorado team believed that they were already well stocked with defensive backs. Once again with the help of his agent Frank Murtha, Carrington signed to play with the Detroit Lions in 1990. Detroit had not won a championship since the '50s, yet the second-year-pro decided to make the best of his circumstances. As a substitute defensive back, Darren played primarily on special teams but was converted from playing corner back to safety. As it later turned out, the position change helped enhance Darren's future in the league. By spring of 1991, Carrington petitioned the NFL league office to become a free agent. Much to Darren's delight, his wishes were granted.

During the 1980s, Bobby Beathard successfully ran the Washington Redskins football club as their general manager. NFL owner Alex Spanos offered the highly regarded Redskins executive the general manager position for the San Diego Chargers. Since the Chargers participated in the same division as Denver, the team knew of Darren's abilities because he had played for the Colorado team. When Carrington's free agency became known, the Chargers expressed interest by signing the young defensive back to a contract with the San Diego club. Darren Carrington's life was about to take yet another turn.

Charger's veteran Gill Byrd had become an established leader of his team's secondary. Years before (in 1983) Byrd was picked by the Chargers in the first round of the NFL draft. As an eight-year NFL veteran, Byrd garnered the respect of his peers and his newest teammate, Darren Carrington. Under Gill's guidance, Darren started to learn more about the ins and outs of playing in the NFL.

Byrd played an important role by influencing Darren in his relationship with Jesus Christ. Gill often shared one of his favorite verses from the Bible, "I am not ashamed of the gospel, because it is the power of God for the salvation of everyone who believes...."[282] With Gill's encouragement, Darren expanded his knowledge of Christianity. With his friend's help, Carrington developed a solid relationship with Jesus Christ. He wanted to be an example to others and not just "a Sunday Christian." [283] It was important for him to follow the teachings of his Savior.

As Darren entered his second year with the Chargers (in 1992), he started to get more playing time as the team's nickel back. That season, Darren received the Charger's Special Team Player of the Year award as a result of his stellar play.

Darren's spiritual changes caused personal changes in his life too. He believed since he and Vickie weren't married, it was inappropriate for them to just live together. After living with Vickie in San Diego for a month, he told the mother of their only child that it would be in their best interest if he moved out. Both of them suffered at this decision. Vickie was the love of his life but..."he knew he wasn't ready spiritually to be the husband and father they deserved." [284]

In order to help his friend, Gill invited Darren to live at his home. Carrington agreed to become a guest at the Byrd household where Gill, his wife and their two boys lived. Here Darren saw firsthand what it meant to be a man of God. Here he learned to live by faith as well as talk about it. Carrington shared how he began to notice that his desires were starting to change as he felt the powerful, loving Christian influence of his friend, Gill Byrd. [285] He also knew that God had chosen Vickie for him. In February of 1993, Darren and Vickie attended a Pro-Athletes Leadership conference. Despite his past doubts, Darren finally knew His Savior loved him unconditionally. Within two months of the conference and after almost a year of premarital counseling, God had given Darren a date to marry the woman he truly loved. [286] On April 10, 1993, Darren and Vickie Carrington were married.

With a clear focus, Darren's playing continued to improve. When he entered his third season with the Chargers, Carrington started as the team's strong safety. His defensive backfield mates included cornerbacks Byrd and Sammy Seale, and Stanley 'The Sheriff' Richard as the team's free safety. The Chargers also had a new coach, Bobby Ross, who sincerely cared for his players. That strong feeling helped create an atmosphere of camaraderie in the Charger locker room which contributed to the team's play that year.

By jumping off to a 6-0 start, San Diego surprised the AFC and even made the cover of Sports Illustrated magazine. Darren and his team enjoyed some national notoriety. The Charger's strong safety also enjoyed a special bundle named Darren II, presented by his wife on October 11, 1994.

Darren's team went on to win the AFC-west title. At the end of the season, the team's first playoff game ended in an exciting 22-21 victory over the visiting Miami Dolphins. The next week, the San Diego club traveled to Pittsburgh to play the Steelers in the AFC title game. With a little more than one minute to play and the Steelers only three yards away from scoring the winning touchdown, Charger's linebacker Dennis Gibson knocked down a Neil O'Donnell pass to seal the victory for the Chargers. Darren and the rest of his Charger teammates were in complete pandemonium. To everyone's surprise, they had just beaten the AFC East Champions (on their turf) to claim the Charger's first AFC crown. On January 15th, the team's bus pulled up to Jack Murphy stadium to be welcomed by over 70,000 screaming and adoring fans. With God's help, Darren had come a long way from his days in the Bronx River projects.

San Diego Chargers participated in their very first Super Bowl at Joe Robbie field in Miami in January '95. They faced a tough NFC opponent—the San Francisco 49ers. The 49ers were arguably the strongest team the NFC had fielded offensively in the game that decade. Sadly, the Charger's winning season came to a halt with a 49-26 loss that night. "There was a general disappointment that the team didn't really give a good showing of what (we) were capable of doing," Darren later explained. [287] The game had been viewed by over 83 million people. Despite the loss, Darren's dream as an eight-year-old boy had come true.

Unfortunately, Darren's friend and mentor, Gill Byrd, wasn't part of the Chargers secondary during that Super Bowl run. Byrd had missed out after an early injury left him on the sidelines. He reminded his friend saying, "Our names will mean nothing someday but God's word will be valuable forever." [288] Darren never forgot that. Somehow he knew that in Gill's absence he'd have to assume a more active spiritual role on the team. He knew more than ever that "God loved Darren Carrington—the man—not just number 29." [289]

As the '95 season approached, NFL owners had added several new teams into the league. Two new franchises, Jacksonville Jaguars and the Carolina Panthers, were allowed to draft a pool of available NFL veterans. Darren was selected to play for his fourth NFL team, the Jacksonville Jaguars. After being initially demoted to second string, Darren eventually worked into being a starter for his new team. Darren also learned a lot about trusting God. The Bible verse Proverbs 3:5-6 became very meaningful to him. It reads: "Trust in the Lord with all your heart. And lean not on your own understanding; in all your ways acknowledge Him, and He shall direct your paths." [290]

During the fourth game, Darren experienced a groin injury that sidelined him. "Physically I was done for the season," he said years later. [291] Even in the violent world of professional football, it's hard for any player to prepare for a season-ending injury. Darren realized that his relationship with Christ was becoming more important to him as each day passed. He knew that he needed God's divine direction more and football less.

By the following year (1996), his agent helped get the NFL veteran a stint with another AFC-West team – the Oakland Raiders. Al Davis, the Raider's majority owner, was cautious but knew Darren's familiarity with his team's common opponents. By the end of spring, Carrington signed on with his fifth NFL team. The Raiders recognized that #29 was a reliable veteran, on a team stocked with veterans.

Darren played with a soft cast during most of the 1996 season as his team's nickel back on defense. The team ended the season with a lackluster 7-9 record and felt that a contract would not be forth coming. By June, 1997, little attention was given to his free agency availability by the other NFL teams. The twenty-nine year old football player felt that this might be it—the end of his NFL career. [292] By summer's end when he didn't hear back from his agent, Darren sadly knew that his NFL career had finished.

Sitting in his office one day, Darren heard the Lord tell him "Because of the career I gave you, you can go ... and tell people about me." [293] Darren's involvement in the Pro Athletes Outreach program let him see just the powerful influence of an athlete. While Darren went about the business of blessing others, God also blessed the couple with their third child, DiJonai on January 8, 1998.

Darren's list of influencers included many noteworthy names. Several years before while still a member of the Chargers, his friend, Gill Byrd, had introduced him to Miles McPherson, a committed Christian who regularly encouraged young athletes to share their faith. McPherson went on to form 'Miles Ahead' and eight years after that he started the Rock Church in San Diego. Darren recalled other positive influences in his life like his two coaches in the projects, his coaches at NAU. Gill Bryd remained the most memorable: the one who taught him about living his faith. Darren realized he could be a positive influence in other people's lives too. As he prayed about an occupation to replace his pro-football career, Darren was asked to join the staff at the Rock Church in Pt. Loma (California) and become their youth pastor.

As Darren grew in wisdom he now understood that achieving a professional football career may give temporary satisfaction but the developing a relationship with Jesus lasts forever. Carrington still finds time to coach his son's high school football team. However, looking back to his early days in the Bronx River projects, he realizes the special journey he has traveled. Darren is especially thankful for the many blessings his family has given him. He is especially grateful for his friendship with his Lord and Savior, Jesus Christ.

Today Darren Carrington is the Family Pastor for the Rock Church in San Diego, California (www.theRockSanDiego.org). He lives in San Diego with his wife Vickie, and their three children, Diarra, Darren, and DiJonai.

While earthly success may feel good, it is only a temporary thing that can fade away quickly. Instead what is most fulfilling is the relationship that each one of us can find with our Creator. Now that is something to cheer about because that's something that lasts for eternity!

Chapter 13

Bryan Maclean Searching for Love

The late '40s and early '50s brought about an unparalleled period of population and economic growth in California. It was during this time on September 25, 1946 that Bryan Andrew Maclean was born in Los Angeles, California. In those days, California was considered the land of opportunity and the destination point for many people who were seeking their own rainbow in the golden state.

Bryan's mother, Elizabeth, was a California native. Around the beginning of World War II she met husband George Maclean. Maclean studied meteorology and later attended architectural school in USC. George enlisted in military service and became a cadet in the United States Air Force. Shortly after the war concluded, Maclean started designing homes for celebrities such as Eddie Fisher and other Hollywood luminaries. [294]

The young Maclean family lived in Hollywood, one of the places to be. Bryan's family routinely found themselves surrounded by members of the movie industry. His mother, Elizabeth (nicknamed "Lizzy") and Bryan lived just a short distance from the Fox Movie Studios and the young boy learned to swim in Elizabeth Taylor's pool. His dad was a friend of actor Robert Stack, who became known for his starring role in the television series, 'The Untouchables' as well as his appearances in over forty films.

Several years later, Elizabeth found herself confronting her husband's womanizing. After a five-year marriage, she filed for divorce and took Bryan to Santa Monica, California.

By 1951, Bryan had a new step-father when Elizabeth married Jack McKee, a licensed contractor. Bryan's stepfather specialized in building new homes during a time of unprecedented growth throughout metropolitan Los Angeles. Jack, Elizabeth, and Bryan moved to west Los Angeles, near Ranch Park.[295]

One day when Bryan was in third grade, Elizabeth received a note from her son's elementary school teacher informing her that they needed to talk. Bryan's teacher told Elizabeth that her son had exceptional musical talent. She encouraged Elizabeth to find a musical instrument for him to play. Even their neighbor, Frederick Lowe (of the Lerner & Lowe composing fame) had once called the young boy a "melodic genius."

Eventually she arranged for Bryan to take piano lessons and he flourished! Elizabeth's confidence in her son's musical ability grew while Bryan still attended Westwood Grammar School. Bryan was selected by the school's music department and a 20th Century Fox representative to sing in the movie, *The Affair to Remember*. The 1957 film starring Cary Grant and Deborah Kerr featured a scene where Bryan sang with other children along with actress Kerr.

Music could always be heard in Bryan's home during his formative years. Broadway hits such as the *West Side Story, Oklahoma,* and *South Pacific*, along with musicals from George and Ira Gershwin just seemed to be the normal sounds coming from the McKee home. The family's love of music further solidified Bryan's intentions to pursue his own aspirations in music.[296]

Bryan also had a strong affinity for folk music and later shared, "As a kid I'd stand in front of the mirror and conduct. I created my own world."[297] Bryan's mom (who had always wanted to find an accompanist to play the guitar while she danced to flamingo music) soon purchased Bryan's first guitar.

Just like many boys his age, Bryan sought the affirmation, love and support of his new father figure, Jack McKee. Jack had a sweet side, but he also had problems controlling his anger. Bryan found it difficult to deal with his step-father's mood swings. [298]

For boys Bryan's age, a place called the Saddle Shop became a favorite hang out and refuge spot for kids around Hollywood. The Saddle Shop sold leather goods and art work to their young clientele. Bryan even occasionally sold some of his own artwork in the store. In that unique social setting, Bryan learned how to play his guitar.

By the time Bryan was in high school, teenagers around Bryan's neighborhood flocked to the popular new musical entertainment club, the Balladeer. There Bryan met the local musician David Crosby who participated in their regular musical line up. David's strong personality, musical skill and his exceptional vocal ability were impressive. Both David and Bryan enjoyed playing folk music, and Crosby soon became another mentor for Bryan. Folk music became popular with the youth from the early to mid-1960's.

Later, Crosby joined the newly formed LA group, the Byrds. Bryan shared, "When I saw the Beatle's movie A Hard Days Night everything changed. I let my hair grow out and I got kicked out of school." [299]

Gaining visibility in the local music scene

As Bryan's musical skills continued to blossom, the teenage guitarist finally got a chance to perform at the Balladeer as a backup guitarist for other musicians. His friendship with Crosby helped him procure a job as road manager for the Bryds and entailed maintaining the group's equipment. He also took charge of setting up the band's sound equipment and helped tune their instruments before each performance. Twenty years later, Bryan looked back fondly on that time. By April of '65, the Byrd's gained a national notoriety with the release of the Dylan penned song, Mr. Tambourine Man.

When the group decided to tour California, they invited Bryan to go along and later Bryan joined part of their first American tour. Disappointment set in when he did not go with them to England. As Bryan later discovered, his exclusion from the English tour was to alter the course of his life.[300]

After being let go as the Byrds' road manager, Bryan went back to playing back-up guitar for musicians at the Balladeer. Because of his past association with the Bryds, Maclean had developed a good reputation in the local music scene.[301]

Arthur Lee, a struggling LA musician, realized this as well. Lee, a Memphis, TN native, was an up-and-coming young Black musician who, like many unknown artists of the time, found himself searching for a musical identity. He found it in a most unusual way; by mixing rock with folk music and later by combining both of these musical expressions with a "punk" music sound. In the documentary movie, Love Story (a film by Start productions), Lee said that one of his (musical) strengths was being able to adapt to a variety (of music styles).[302]

Bryan first met Arthur Lee in the parking lot at Ben Frank's coffee shop. He shared how Arthur had invited him to come and hear Lee's band at the Brave New World, an entertainment club in Los Angeles. "For some reason, (Arthur) ended up in my car. He needed to get somewhere and I said I'd drive him. And that was the beginning of our friendship." Lee was already playing in a band with friend Johnny Echols, the group's lead guitarist.

Arthur invited Bryan to join his group, the Grassroots. Lee felt convinced that Bryan's talent would help boost the group's following. The group kept track of the Byrds progress, as they had recently bolstered their popularity with the release of Pete Seeger's penned song, Turn, Turn, Turn. The Grassroots were searching for that same kind of success.

Bryan and his mates liked their new band's sound. The nineteen-year old eagerly became a part of this diverse rock group that featured a black lead guitarist (Johnny Echols), a white bass player (Ken Fossi), a black lead singer (Arthur Lee) and white drummer (Snoopy Pfsiter) who had played for The Safaris' 1963 hit, Wipe Out.

Bryan became the band's rhythm guitarist. As music critic Andrew Sandoval later wrote, Bryan's entry into the group "would not only complete the band's line-up but (would) also add that intangible quality that made the group magical."[303]

During the mid-1960s, rock music was exploding in popularity. In Hollywood; Arthur, Bryan, Johnny, Ken and Snoopy's band quickly became one of the more popular street bands in Hollywood. The band developed a strong following especially among those who frequented the local entertainment clubs such as Bido Lito's, The Whiskey and others. The band often played to hundreds of fans crammed inside a small club, with hundreds more packing the streets outside.

Arthur and the rest of his band mates soon realized that they had to create another stage name when rumors were confirmed that another local band was using their Grassroots name. Without a record contract and a manager advising them, Arthur, Johnny, Bryan, Ken and Snoopy had to make this next step.

The group decided to have their fans choose their new name. During a performance one night, Arthur provided some suggestions to their fans. One suggestion was simply Love. The audience enthusiastically shouted their approval and Love became their new name. Even Bryan was pleased, and overnight, the band's name went from the Grassroots to Love.

In the early 1960s, Elektra Records made it big on the East coast. Their founder, Jac Holzman, continuously searched for exciting new acts. This New York based company had a reputation for featuring folk artists as the mainstay of their lineup. After a decade in business, the company had begun to expand into other genres of music. By 1965, the company released their first blues album featuring a group from Chicago's east side, calling themselves, the Paul Butterfield Blues Band.

Holzman had also heard of some fresh new music groups that were making their way around the Los Angeles area. Much to his delight, the record company executive discovered tremendous local fan support for Love. He witnessed the phenomenon on the streets of Hollywood and at the entertainment clubs around town. The recording company signed Arthur, Bryan, Johnny, Ken and Snoopy to their first record contract. Love was on its way! [304]

Arthur bought himself a Mercedes sports car with the $5000 cash signing bonus fee he received from the contract. Through his contacts in Hollywood, Bryan arranged for the band to stay at the Hollywood mansion of Bela Lugosi (of Dracula legend). They affectionately named it the castle.

LA's newest recording artists started putting together their first record album. By March (1966), Elektra released the band's first single, My Little Red Book. The song "was a raw adaptation of Burt Bacharach and Hal David's (composition) ...Bacharach was reportedly furious with Love's hard-edged rendition" of the song.[305]

Some of the songs on Love's first album were written in collaboration. Bryan's song, Softly to Me, which he also sang solo, was included in the fourteen-track release. The debut record reached No. 57 on the charts, selling over 150,000 copies.[306]

The group's songwriting was prolific while living at the castle between 1966 and 1967. Even Bryan admitted these were the best song-writing years of his life. Love used the mansion to rehearse songs for their upcoming album, Da Capo. The castle became known as 'the place' where rock musicians would gather. Members of groups such as Jefferson Airplane, Janis Joplin, Jimi Hendrix Experience and The Doors visited or even stayed there. Bryan remembers Arthur becoming particularly annoyed one day with a young singer who interrupted the band's practice session with his drug-induced antics and swam naked in the mansion's pool. Arthur decided to remove the man from the residence. Bryan wanted to better acquaint himself with the unknown singer from the group that called themselves the Doors. The mysterious young man was none other than Jim Morrison, their lead singer.[307]

Love went back to the studio to record their second single, 7 and 7 Is by June 1966. The song released in July and reached # 33 on the 'Billboard top 40' chart. Arthur decided to add two musicians to the band; Tray Cantrelli to play flute and saxophone and Michael Stuart replacing Pfisterer on drums. Pfisterer was switched to organ and harpsichord. 'Snoopy' had been a concert pianist in his early days so this move proved to be genius.

Love completed their second album, Da Capo (meaning back to the beginning) released in 1967. The album included an eighteen-minute song that took up all of side B. The release also contained a variety of classic originals such as Orange Skies, Stephanie Knows Who, Que Vida, and She Comes in Colors. [308]

Tragically, Bryan and the rest of the band got caught up in the use of drugs and alcohol. Holzman expressed his sorrow in an interview years later regarding the band's substance abuse problems. Drugs were so prevalent that Bryan's mom once complained saying, "There always was a hash pipe in a room at the group's residence at the castle." In one out-take recording (released many years later by Rhino Records) Arthur accused a band member of "blowing" during a session. Some believe that this explains why the group avoided regular tours.

Like most other recording labels, Elektra wanted to see their newest album releases (like Da Capo) supported by regional or national tours by their bands. Unfortunately for Elektra and their fans, Arthur expressed reluctance to tour. The band started losing its cohesiveness and began to show signs of falling apart. By the next summer (1967) Arthur, Johnny, Bryan, Snoopy and Ken were no longer living together. Despite their difficulties, Bryan and Love were offered some promising professional opportunities. Unfortunately, Arthur seemed to have a different agenda and turned down an invitation for the band to play at the Monterey Pop Festival. Monterey Pop became a legendary 1960s music festival. Organized by John Phillips of Mamas and Papas fame, the festival became one of the key music events which ignited the professional careers of pop legends such as Janis Joplin, Jimi Hendrix and bands like the Who. Years later Arthur admitted that it had been a mistake for him to turn down Phillip's invitation to perform at the legendary festival.

By the summer of 1967, the remaining members of the band worked in the studio on their third album, Forever Changes. Arthur, along with the album's producers decided to bring in professional studio musicians to record the first two cuts of the record. By early June, Andmoreagain and The Daily Planet were recorded in the same fashion. The rest of the band was disappointed with Lee's decision to use studio musicians and became more determined than ever to show up and perform to everyone's highest expectations.

Both Arthur's and Bryan's compositions were unlike anything they had put on vinyl before. Arthur's admitted 'gift of variety' was pivotal in organizing the music for their new album. Bryan had two compositions that were included in the final cut of the new release. Bryan's song, Old Man, might have been a reflection on his own past and the personal longing for the close father-son relationship he never had. It is also possible that there could have been some spiritual references in the song as well. Bryan's band mate Johnny Echols told writer Andrew Sandoval "At the time I don't think Bryan really realized his beliefs ... He was kind of searching, looking."

It's generally recognized that Bryan's masterpiece composition of the album, Alone Again set the tone for the new album. Arthur provided the strong vocals on the first song (side A) mixed with a string and horn accompaniment. The orchestral arrangement of the song pleased him. Alone Again or was completed by September of 1967. However, the relationship between the band's leader and his original band mates remained strained.

The majority of the other nine tracks on the album were complicated pieces and very challenging. Many of the third album's compositions were unusual by rock standards making it the critic's choice some forty years later. Rolling Stone Magazine recognized the album as one of the top forty rock albums <u>ever made.</u>

However, upon its release in 1968, Forever Changes received lackluster reviews. Bryan told his mother that he was "disillusioned that they didn't tour." He felt they missed a golden opportunity to demonstrate their talents. Forever Changes is now regarded as a classic; a musical masterpiece of its era. Jeff Weis, a Los Angeles music critic said that of all of the talented groups that came from Los Angeles, perhaps Love was the best. They were "the least commercially successful but arguably the greatest ... whose reputation rests largely on the strength of one perfect document: Forever Changes." Weis said the band's third album was "perhaps the most quintessentially Los Angeles record there is" ... "Love's picture of Los Angeles is very much a native vision ... (It is) "a seamless summation of the town's ... myriad complexities." [309]

It had taken a supreme effort for the band to collaborate on the album. Bryan somehow felt disconnected with Lee, in part because most of his material remained overlooked in the studio. Jac Holzman recognized Bryan's musical ability and decided to offer him the opportunity of branching out on his own. By spring of 1968, Bryan decided to leave the group. Bryan later admitted to writer David Fricke, "I wasn't ready to launch out on my own … I couldn't be a Tim Buckley."

The years of drug use had taken a toll on Bryan. "Bryan had an addiction to heroin at this point in his life and had a near death experience when he overdosed after leaving Love." Gone were the days of the camaraderie of playing together in the clubs, and the good times at the castle.[310] By 1968 The original band that many believed had so much potential, so much promise simply fell apart.

By 1969 Bryan left for New York. He decided to take Holzman's offer to record his compositions for a new solo album. While Bryan had some wonderful compositions, his studio work wasn't well received by the record company decision makers. According to his mother, "Bryan didn't get along well with the studio musicians in New York … He was out of it." Elizabeth attributes this, in part, to the drinking problems her son had. Ultimately the label decided to pass on releasing Bryan's solo work. His mother believed that this rejection had a devastating effect on her son and only intensified his drinking problem.[311]

Searching for Meaning

Bryan wasn't the only one stumbling around in the world. His mother Elizabeth was searching for the meaning of life as well when her daughter, five-year-old Maria McKee surprised her one day. Elizabeth was picking Maria up from her small Baptist school when Maria looked up into her mother's eyes and said, "Momma, I love Jesus." Maria's profession of faith in Christ deeply touched her mom. Elizabeth shared, "I needed a change too; I felt desperate."

While watching local television a few weeks later, Elizabeth providentially came across a Billy Graham telecast that intrigued her. For the first time she heard the gospel and the plan of salvation. She said that the famous evangelist gave a message that was easy to understand. That night in front of her television set, Elizabeth McKee bowed her head and asked Jesus Christ to be Lord and Savior of her life. It was a simple act of faith but it would ultimately have profound effects. Bryan's mother started attending a small Baptist church in west Los Angeles and even started meeting with other ladies to regularly pray for their closest relatives.[312]

After his initial disappointment in New York City (NYC) the year before, Bryan decided to make another attempt to resurrect his music career. Maclean tried to record with Capitol records but no new record deal was forthcoming. One evening when he was in a bar on Third Avenue (in New York City) Bryan started sipping a glass of beer. Suddenly the taste became so bitter and sour he couldn't finish his glass. He had reached the end. Feeling hopeless and full of despair, the young musician cried out to something greater than drugs, alcohol or himself. He emptied his heart and told God about his pain, hurts, disappointments, addictions and got real about his mess of a life. That night Bryan felt a touch from heaven.

"Lizzy" got an early surprise from her son the Christmas of 1970 when he showed up without notice on her door step. After hugging and greeting his mom, Bryan showed Elizabeth the first few pages of his Bible. He proudly showed his surprised mother the page where he had signed a written commitment to his new Savior, Jesus Christ. Elizabeth was overcome with joy. God had answered her prayers! Her son had finally welcomed his mom's best friend, Jesus Christ, to be the Lord and Savior of his life.[313]

Though every day seemed new and exciting, it was still difficult for Bryan to cope with not being a rock star any more. He soon decided to go back to school and get his high school degree. Bryan lived with his mother, stepfather and sister, Maria for the next three years. Together, they attended a small Baptist church on Sundays. Bryan even helped the church by driving kids to Sunday school. After several years, Bryan began to feel out of place at the church. As a former rock musician, he still struggled to adjust to this different environment.[314]

During the mid '70s Bryan became involved in running The Daisy, a Christian coffee house in Beverly Hills. The club had some success. Solo recording artists such as Oden Fong fondly remembered meeting Bryan when he played there. Bryan even considered getting involved in full time ministry when the music club finally closed. Still, his commitment to music remained as strong as ever. He believed his music to be a God-given gift that he still needed to share.

Arthur invited Bryan to participate in a ten-year reunion of his old group, Love, in 1978. Bryan nixed the idea of a tour to England with Love when he found out he hadn't been paid for an earlier performance. Still, Maclean wouldn't give up his quest to revive his music career.

For the next fifteen years, Bryan held a variety of jobs but nothing seemed to compete with his strong desire to be a professional musician and composer. He wrote a variety of music during this time, from worship music to country. He even tried to professionally form a music duo with his sister, Maria McKee. The compact disc No One Was Kinder celebrates that short collaboration. Maria went on to become an accomplished song writer, in her own right, penning two # 1 hits besides participating in several movie soundtracks. (For more information to go: www.MariaMcKeeinfo.com.)

During the '80's Bryan penned another big hit. Don't Toss Us Away, and it reached # 1 on the charts. It was a huge hit for country recording artist Patty Loveless. It also helped restore some of the confidence Bryan had lost and brought him some financial success.

Despite the success of the song, Bryan still struggled with substance abuse. His addictions pulled him down into a very dark pit of despair. His mother Elizabeth (who worked at a Vineyard Church in Orange County) began to feel increasingly burdened for her son's physical well being. When Elizabeth found out that the unit below her son's apartment in Hollywood was available for rent, she moved in.

Overcoming Addiction

After sharing her concerns with her son, Bryan decided to enter a program that had great success in treating people with substance abuse. For years, Victory Outreach (VO) ministries has had a great reputation in dealing with people who had problems with either alcohol or drug abuse. They had outreach centers all over the world.

Bryan participated in their program for almost fifteen months, and it altered his life dramatically. The demons of drug and alcohol dependency left him. For the first time in years, Bryan felt delivered and free. [315]

After undergoing this intensive rehabilitation program, Bryan decided to move back to his apartment in Hollywood. He celebrated his new freedom by frequently jogging to Griffith Park early each morning. His mother remembered her son getting up every day at dawn and running the two and a half miles to the park observatory. (Griffith Park had become famous years earlier from several scenes from the 1955 cult movie classic, Rebel Without a Cause starring James Dean and Natalie Wood). Bryan regularly scaled the large hill, and when he reached the top he would pray each morning. He found it a great place to get away from the hustle and bustle of the streets of LA. [316]

With new vigor, he began to compose praise and worship songs. Bryan derived much joy from this kind of writing, and his newly inspired faith in Christ became the focal point in his life. He wanted to musically express just how he felt, and by 1998, the fifty-four-year-old musician put the finishing touches on Intramurals, his definitive recording (disc) release. [317]

On Christmas day, 1998, Bryan Andrew Maclean went home to be with Jesus. His weary heart just gave out. Bryan's untimely death was a shock to those around him. Those closest to him speculated that the years of substance abuse had taken their toll on the talented musician. On January 9th, 1999 his friends, relatives and neighbors remembered the man who once said, "Jesus was compared to an eagle. He was compared to a lion and I want to be like Him."

Today Bryan is still missed by many who knew him and many more who know him only by his music. Even though Bryan is now in heaven, his recordings and songs of worship still live on with us. While God gives each of us various talents, what we do with those talents is our responsibility and gift to Him. Bryan made the most

Chapter 14

Brenda M. MacKillop A Playboy Bunny Finds Peace

W hen we view ourselves in the mirror, we see might not like the image that we see glancing back at us.To be sure, that image is not necessarily how others see us and it certainly is not how our Creator beholds us. Brenda lost sight of her true self for a number of years.

A most beautiful baby girl entered the world May 28, 1950. Her father Elmer, a longshoreman, loved the water and became the captain of a tugboat. Brenda's mother, Joyce, enjoyed her role as a homemaker and took care of Brenda and her siblings in their Norfolk, VA home.

During Brenda's early childhood, life was tense and at times traumatic due to her parent's frequent arguments. Brenda, a shy, sensitive and introverted child, was affected by the turmoil in the home. She took it to heart when her father threatened her mom by telling her that if she got fat he would divorce her.[318] The stress between the couple escalated when Elmer started drinking. Brenda summed up her childhood by explaining that "life at home was a constant hell."[319]

Over time, Brenda became increasingly convinced that her mother disliked her daughters and gave preferential treatment to her two brothers. Also the fact that her father kept stacks of old Playboy magazines lying around the house became just one more thing that disturbed the troubled young girl.

The eleven year old did find some solace when her mother took her to church each week. During a Baptist revival in 1961, Brenda asked Christ to come into her heart. Even with her new religious experience, Brenda did not fully comprehend what a personal relationship with Jesus Christ entailed. While Brenda regularly participated in traditional prayers during supper and would even recite the Lord's Prayer with friends at school, she didn't really understand the Bible. Furthermore, she had no one to teach or mentor her in her new faith.

As the young teenager transitioned from Blair Junior High School to Maury High in Norfolk, she started experimenting with horoscopes and fortune telling. Brenda was unaware that the Bible discouraged this type of behavior. Brenda marginalized her personal conduct when she began sleeping around with a high school boyfriend. She justified herself calling it acceptable "because the Bible was written a long time ago for people who got married very young." [320]

Brenda had no parental support at home and sought peer approval in other areas of her life. After getting good grades through high school, Brenda assumed that her parents would financially assist her with her college education. After a while Brenda realized her parents had other plans and she became deeply despondent. She just couldn't understand why they were willing to help her brothers but refused to help her. [321]

Off to College

Brenda felt overjoyed with her acceptance to Old Dominion University. She now found herself spending sleepless nights desperately thinking of ways to raise money so she could attend the local college. Brenda discovered that she could earn scholarship money by winning beauty pageants. The top three finishers of the events received college scholarships.

Brenda's beauty turned heads wherever she went. She entered the Junior Miss Pageant held in Norfolk and placed first runner up. She won the scholarship money she desperately needed! Soon afterwards, she became first runner up in another contest; for the title of Miss

Norfolk, again winning more scholarship money. That same summer, Brenda Miller won the "Miss Smile" contest sponsored by the Coca Cola Company, Kodak, United Airlines, Jansen clothing and Kauai Surf resorts. Her success in these events boosted her confidence.[322]

Brenda entered Old Dominion University and selected a psychology major. With her freshman year ending that next summer of 1969, money again became a priority for the pretty young college student. During the summer of 1969, Brenda decided to accept an offer from the sponsors of the "Miss Smile" pageant and travel to Hawaii to work as a social hostess for Kauai Surf Resorts. This gave her enough money to continue her sophomore year at school but instead Brenda chose to pursue employment with a local Hawaiian Resort because she had so enjoyed being away from home for the first time in her life.

Personal Tragedy

While looking for employment with the human resource department of a local Waikiki Beach resort, the HR representative asked her out on a date. Desperate for work, she reluctantly accepted. Years later, Brenda looks back at this moment as an unwise decision. Tragically, she was raped that evening.

The nineteen-year-old girl felt terrified and alone. She had no one to turn to and no place to go. She felt abandoned by her parents, and like most rape victims, she didn't tell anyone about what had happened. Within a few weeks after her attack she found employment at a local bank.

Brenda decided to return home in December 1969 by using the other half of the round trip ticket provided by Inter-Island resorts. She developed a relationship with a photographer and he proposed to her. She declined and felt even more determined to re-enroll at the university and pursue her degree. Brenda's mother allowed her to share her car, however, money continued to be an issue. She went to work at a modeling agency which helped replace some of her dwindling finances.[323]

Brenda's relationship with her mother continued to deteriorate as Joyce's indifference towards the girl became even more transparent.

On one occasion, Brenda and her mother got into a horrific argument. Joyce finally admitted her deep contempt for her daughter and they got into a fight. Joyce was furious and screamed at her daughter, "Get out and never darken my doorway again."[324]

With tears streaming down her face at this total rejection, Brenda left. Brenda's cousin offered to take her in until she could figure out what to do. Brenda felt confused and had absolutely no direction in her life. While she would occasionally seek advice from friends, she became more determined than ever to find peace and happiness on her own terms. Eventually Brenda found a job as a receptionist and later as a customer service representative for a local auto dealer. During this time, she began dating and sleeping around town with a series of both married and unmarried men.

The Beauty Pageant Scene

Again the former model looked to the pageant circuit as a way of getting scholarship money so she could resume her education. In May of 1971 Brenda entered and won the Miss Virginia pageant. As her state's pageant representative, Brenda was invited to be a contestant in the Miss USA beauty pageant several weeks later.

The Miss Virginia pageant winner was on top of the world! Her ascendancy to the most famous beauty pageant in the country helped her cope with her self esteem problems. She even hoped that her entrance into the (Miss USA) pageant would win back some of her parent's love and approval.[325]

The Miss USA pageant finished the season with Brenda placing in the top twelve out of the fifty contestants and being selected as the most photogenic contestant in the pageant. For the next twelve months, Brenda did promotion work on behalf of her state. She also became involved in a number of public relations jobs including representing the Holiday Inn.

During this time, the movie The Last Detail was being filmed in Norfolk, Virginia. This 1973 film stared actors Jack Nicholson, Randy Quaid and Otis Young. There she met a member of the film's production crew. Brenda met a new boy friend who became so enamored with the Virginia pageant winner that he asked her to move to Los Angeles and live with him.

Moving to Hollywood

The thought of moving to Hollywood intrigued Brenda. With new contacts, a new life, and a new environment in front of her, she truly thought she might be able to make something of herself. With those thoughts, Brenda moved to California in 1973.

Not long after she arrived in LA, she learned that Playboy was opening one of their clubs in Century City, Los Angeles. (Yes, this was the very same magazine that her father had left scattered around the house when she was younger.)

The Playboy Clubs were "staffed by ... Bunnies, spurred by the sexual revolution, (and) spanned the globe in their heyday in the 1960s and '70s, from Chicago and New York to Manila, London, Tokyo and the Bahamas. At their height, 22 clubs were in operation ... boasting more than a million 'key holders' or members."[326] After working for a temporary agency and on her own in a strange, new city Brenda hoped that her Hollywood contacts could help advance her entry into the film industry.

"Needing work, Brenda learned from a friend that the Playboy Club was having a 'bunny hunt' to get new girls."[327] Judi Bradford, representing the Club, offered the former Miss Virginia a job as a 'Bunny' waitress. "Of the 600 girls who applied, she was one of the thirty who were selected."[328] Brenda still thought her future rested in being discovered by someone in the Hollywood film industry. She believed that this new job would enhance her prospects of getting into the entertainment business.

Brenda's persistence paid off. She accepted a job as an extra in the best-selling film, Godfather II and even had a small speaking role as a showgirl in Las Vegas. However, the Bunny job still remained Brenda's main source of income over the next three years and there were perks. Her job reinforced her licentious attitude toward sex and relationships with men. The Century City Club was a beacon for the 'sexually liberated' lifestyle embraced by many progressives during the '70s.

During her first six weeks at the club, Brenda received training from her employer as a 'Bunny' and club waitress. On Sundays, however, she regularly attended a local Presbyterian Church and bragged that she worked for the club.

Brenda's life seemed to be full of contradictions. As she "worked at the Playboy Club bar, she was surrounded by the Playmate Gallery, a display of nude centerfolds. Men would leer at the pornographic pictures and then ask if (she) was up there... (She) felt these men had no respect for women with their only interest seemed to be in satisfying their lust." [329] Nevertheless, meeting celebrities at the famous Los Angeles Playboy Club in the 70's was just another perk of being a Bunny. On opening night of the Club, Brenda Miller was given the honor of serving Hugh Hefner and his guests at her assigned table.

Hugh Hefner, founder and majority shareholder of Playboy Magazine, had a variety of holdings. They included television entertainment programming as well as ownership in the Playboy clubs around the world. Just like many Bunnies who worked with her, Brenda heard stories about Hefner's mansion and his infamous swing parties. Brenda discovered many of these rumors to be true.

It didn't take long for Brenda to become engulfed in the Playboy lifestyle. The magazine's publisher rigorously promoted the magazine's lifestyle along with the amoral philosophy featured in his magazine. Hefner's magazine routinely belittled Christianity, traditional morality and social restraints on sex. "What non-consumers (of the magazine) do not know is that Playboy has always been much more than a 'girlie' or 'men's magazine.' It has long been a bully pulpit for a world view that judges men according to their tally of sexual conquests." [330]

"Trumpeting the Kinseyian ideology since 1953, Hefner and Playboy insisted marital love alone was not sufficient for healthy sexuality." [331] Brenda soon discovered how true this was for her fellow Playboy party friends and acquaintances.

Finally the former Miss Virginia was invited by the publisher's secretary to attend the mansion's regular Sunday afternoon party.

As a precaution, she decided to talk to some of her friends from work about her reluctance to attend. One friend told her, "It was nice to dine on Beef Wellington and see the latest PG or R movies ... Nevertheless (Brenda) was afraid people would be walking around nude ... but this wasn't the case – at least not on Sunday afternoons, so (she) decided to give it a try." [332]

Brenda attended her first mansion party in 1973 which featured a showing of a current run Hollywood film. Eventually Brenda was invited to attend the mid-week parties that included some wild sex orgies.

Brenda met a number of well known celebrities and explained, "It was exciting to think that these important famous men wanted (her). There were many other celebrities that (she) hobnobbed with, but it took her quite a while to make one important discovery." [333] As the twenty-four-year old Virginian continued to work for 'the Club,' she came to feel that "many men would come to the Playboy Club with the idea of purchasing sex." [334] Since bunnies were routinely encouraged by Club management to find new 'key' holders, Brenda believed her 'sex' appeal to be her only value.

She soon discovered, "it wasn't really me, a person with feeling, ideas, desires, dreams, a soul that they (the celebrities) wanted to have a relationship with. I was only another attractive body that they could use for their lustful pleasures." [335] They offered her special tips just to go to bed with some of their male customers. While she didn't participate in this form of prostitution, she did meet with celebrities and other prosperous friends to have sex during Hefner's parties.

At this juncture, Brenda's life took a downward spiral. Looking back, Brenda remembers, "I saw marijuana being used at Hefner's mansion on a regular basis and cocaine as well" (AG Commission). Brenda also shared about taking amounts of alcohol and prescription tranquilizers thinking it would do no harm, but "how the lust just grows with more drugs and alcohol to desensitize the psyche for sexual perversions." [336]

Brenda's promiscuous lifestyle started catching up with her. She went to a wild sex party one night and then went to church Sunday morning. The two lifestyles were playing tug of war. Brenda became increasingly depressed because she believed that men were only interested in having sex. She openly shared, "It was this lack of caring, loving and commitment in a relationship that caused (her) depression and hopelessness to worsen." [337]

The young woman found herself immersed in a lifestyle careening out of control. Brenda lived the fast, sex and alcohol induced lifestyle that, in the '70s, was idolized by her employer's flagship enterprise, Playboy Magazine. She felt miserable!

The magazine's promiscuous philosophy of sexual freedom seemed to have no bounds. The American University (in Washington D.C.) completed a study which showed the negative effects that soft porn publications such as Playboy have on the culture. The study showed during the 1970s that Playboy published a number of controversial 'drug education' cartoons and images of young children, grandmothers, women and parents all partaking of marijuana. These cartoons and images clearly demonstrate how the publication subtly promotes these controversial viewpoints. Is it any wonder that in 1979, a representative from Playboy responded to a Chicago television station's assertion that the magazine was corrupting America's morality by saying, "I certainly hope so!"

Recovering From a Nightmare Life

Living in this nightmare, Brenda soon realized that her promiscuous lifestyle was turning her into an amoral and totally corrupt woman. Her depression had spiraled to new lows and thoughts of suicide crept into her mind daily. Brenda recalled one holiday season with clarity. "It was Christmas Eve of 1975, the lights were blinking on the tree laden with angel ornaments, and I was looking forward to finding peace in heaven as the gas poured out of my oven in my Beverly Hills apartment. How long, I wondered, would it take to die by gas? Would I just go to sleep and never wake up? Or would I choke on my own vomit as I had heard those do when one overdoses on alcohol and pills?" [338] Her deep pain and depression were pulling her down a road closer and closer to death.

Fortunately for Brenda she didn't die that night. Her current boyfriend, a professional comedian, came to her apartment that evening bearing gifts only to find his dazed girlfriend near death's door. Brenda's boyfriend, (who was married), opened the windows and shut off the gas, thwarting her holiday suicide attempt. [339]

In the fall of '76, she sprained her ankle at work by slipping on some water. As she started collecting workman's compensation checks, she found herself again battling the feelings of depression that had haunted her for the past several years. Homebound and isolated, her emotional state deteriorated. She finally decided to move back to Virginia where she still continued to collect disability.

Depression continued to plague her and she overdosed on a mixture of tranquilizers and alcohol. She later described the episode to a reporter from a Christian magazine recalling, "I became overwhelmed with the fear of dying and decided instead to call an ambulance service. The doctor at the emergency room emptied my stomach and assigned me to spend time at the local mental health hospital."

After having surgery to repair the damaged tendons in her ankle, Brenda Miller decided to change her lifestyle. While recovering from her battles with depression, she started the search for a new job. She ran into an old friend and acquaintance, Nina Visocky, who offered to share an apartment over a warehouse. For the next several months, Brenda found herself recovering from all the brokenness she'd experienced in Los Angeles. She knew, without a doubt, that she could no longer continue to live recklessly. She reflected on that 1961 Baptist revival and all the religious influence in her life. Only God could rescue her from this black hole of depression. Brenda said, "I wanted to find love, purpose and meaning in life and not just be a sexual play toy any more."

Almost by 'accident', Brenda ran into an old friend who worked for the Christian Broadcasting Network in Norfolk (VA), and he hired her. [340] The initial contact eventually led to an assignment as a production assistant for CBN. (Isn't it amazing how one random meeting can cause a person to turn a corner and change their life's entire direction?) There truly are no coincidences in life!

Over time Brenda developed a keen interest in reading the Bible cover to cover. She now felt her life finally beginning to turn around. She laid her shattered past at the foot of the Cross and with the only true Savior who loved her unconditionally.

One day, Stan Majkut, a director at CBN, invited her to attend The Rock Church located in Virginia Beach. Soon she became a member of the Church, which was composed of 3,000 on- fire, Spirit-filled Christians. [341] Brenda's involvement with this church was to have a profound, pivotal and positive effect on her life. One Sunday, as Brenda went forward for prayer, she made the decision to completely surrender to God. From that moment, she experienced deliverance from the suicidal demons that had haunted her since her teenage days. She would admit years later, "I always knew He existed but I never knew He loved me and would forgive me." Brenda recognized that "God gently and kindly delivered me." [342] She also knew that her walk with Christ represented a brand new direction in her life. She had finally found the peace that had eluded her all these years.

Brenda's job with CBN provided a challenging and rewarding experience. She wrote, directed and produced interviews for The 700 Club. While on an assignment with CBN, Brenda traveled to Chicago in December of 1979 to fulfill a speaking engagement the CBN production assistant had with a local church. During this engagement Brenda met Raymond MacKillop, a correspondent for a local Christian TV station. Brenda and Ray saw each other again the next day when she interviewed Raymond's manager for a television piece she was doing for CBN.

Over the course of the next four months, Raymond and Brenda saw each other in various cities around the eastern seaboard. These once-a-month (business) meetings would culminate when Raymond proposed to her on April 28, 1980.

The couple married on September 21, 1980. Today the MacKillop's have three children; Mark (1981), Amy Gail (1985) and Raymond David (1985). Brenda successfully earned an Associate of Science in Nursing Degree from Purdue University, and four years later, her Bachelors of Science degree in nursing at Valparasio University. [343]

Raymond MacKillop has now faithfully served as the Senior Pastor of the Shiloh Assembly of God in San Pierre, Indiana for over twenty-six years. The MacKillops continue to serve God together. Brenda is reminded everyday that the same loving God who rescued her can rescue anyone who sincerely reaches out to Him.

To this day, Brenda continues to be in awe of the depth of God's love for each of us. Because of her remarkable story, she knows without a doubt that the God she serves sees each one of us as a unique individual, not as an airbrushed image or an object of pleasure perpetuated by the Playboy philosophy. It has become especially clear to Brenda that while mankind may look at the outward appearance of a person, God has the divine insight of seeing one's heart.

Chapter 15

Patricia Louise White Escaping the "Great Deception"

W hat is truth? You can't touch it, feel it, smell it but you can hear it. Somehow you know in your heart when you have heard the real Truth. While others might try to lead you astray, your heart knows better.

Born March 22, 1931 in Pana, Illinois, Patricia Louise Morrison was the second of five children. Patricia grew up in humble yet loving surroundings. Pat's father, Frank Pierpoint Morrison, was a blue collar worker yet had an unusual appreciation for poetry, classic opera and violin music. Frank's wife, Erma Lorene, enjoyed reading and taught school. Both parents made an effort to teach their five children (Sharolyn, Patricia, Tony, Freddy and Lee) the importance of being honest and polite. On Sundays, Erma Lorene always found the time to take her young children to church.[344]

By the time Patricia was four years old, the family moved from Illinois to New York. Although America was recovering from the worst years of the Great Depression with unemployment still high, Frank was able to find work in Long Island constructing green houses.

As the Second World War began in the early '40s, Americans were asked to sacrifice a great deal and rationing cards further limited everyone's use of many of the basic staples. Frank decided to sell the family car and use public transportation. He reasoned that the kids could walk to school, he lived close to work, and if they had to go to

New York City, it was only thirty minutes away. The family enjoyed their hometown of Sayville which was described by Pat as a lovely town on the South Bay. [345]

August 15, 1945 came, marking the end of the WWII and brought about celebrations all over Pat's hometown and other communities throughout the country. Everyone's emotions, including the Morrison family were running high that day. It was a day that remained etched in Patricia's mind as one of thanksgiving that the world-wide conflict had finally ended.

When Pat turned sixteen, she took a part-time job as a waitress to help supplement her family's income as she continued her studies in school. During her early high school years Patricia started attending the Antonini Dance Studio and even played the lead role in her school's play during her senior year. In June of 1949, Patricia graduated from Sayville High School. She attributed her love of dance to the influence of her music teacher Ms. Davidson. [346] Eventually Pat's passion in the field led her into teaching ballet and to dance professionally for a number of years. She occasionally took a class in piano, dance, drama or other fields of study she enjoyed.

About eight years later, Pat met her future husband, John W. White, while attending a local Methodist Church. A year and a half later she truly danced for joy when they married on July 9, 1960. As a graduate of the University of Georgia, Patricia's husband worked as a field assistant for United Airlines.

Pat and John's daughter, Leslie, was born and again Patricia's heart danced for joy. The couple adopted their second child, Beth, eight years later. As a mother of two young children, Pat gave the appearance of a happy, well adjusted woman. Yet, somehow Patricia felt something missing. She thought that she had somehow lost opportunities. With issues of low self esteem, Pat believed, that "Everyone else was better than I was". [347] While Pat, John and the family regularly attended the local Methodist church, she admitted years later, "I believed in God but I had no concept of who He was, especially about Jesus. The Holy Spirit was a complete mystery to me." [348]

An Experience with Mormonism

Four years later Patricia and John purchased a home in Alexandria, Virginia. The move was necessitated by a transfer from John's employer. The family still enjoyed vacationing up north and when New York City served as hostess for the 1964 World's Fair, they took in the sights. [349] The six-month fair was held on Long Island from April to October that year. It brought in millions of dollars and tourists from around the world.

One particular pavilion at the fair intrigued Pat and John White. The exhibit offered by the Church of the Latter Day Saints (LDS) appeared spectacular. Like the LDS church's ongoing exhibit at their Temple in Salt Lake City, the World's Fair exhibit introduced people to Mormonism in an elaborate way. The Church's President, David McKay said the exhibit was "one of the most unique and effective missionary efforts in [the Church's] history." [350] Impressed by the pavilion's large, color murals of the church's Prophets' and Biblical characters from the Old Testament times, Patricia spent an inordinate amount of time there. They also watched a short film, Man's Search for Happiness. At the end of their visit to the pavilion, Pat gave her name to the Mormon officials at the exhibit, indicating her interest in learning more about their religion.

Sure enough, an Elder from the local LDS Church arranged for a series of meetings with Pat and John in their home. After several meetings with the church's missionaries, Pat accepted the teaching of the Mormon Church as credible.

Pat vividly recalled hearing with her own ears an audible male voice telling her, "This is true." Pat even asked her husband, "did you hear the voice?' She wanted a confirmation that she had heard a voice while talking with the LDS missionaries. Puzzled by her question, Pat's husband responded by asking, "What voice?" Pat remained convinced she had received a directive from heaven representing the truth. That voice had a vice grip on John's wife for the next twenty years of her life. [351]

Patricia felt the Mormon Church provided her with the comfort and assurances that she hadn't found at the Methodist Church.

Impressed with the high regard of the Mormon Church for family, the young Mormon mother became very involved with her local ward. Pat learned from her Mormon Elders and teachers that Christian denominations, over a period of many years, had abandoned the original tenants of the Church. The priesthood authority, according to her LDS officials, had been lost along with the Old Testament administration of the priesthood duties.

The historical founder of the Church of the Latter Day Saints, Joseph Smith had once had a vision from God. Smith told his followers that his vision revealed how other churches and religious creeds were an abomination to God.[352] "He was told that none of the churches on earth had the fullness of the truth. Over time, Joseph Smith was chosen to establish Christ's Church and restore the priesthood or the authority to act in God's name." [352]

By the following year (1965) Pat and John were baptized into their local LDS ward. John was promoted to church leadership and eventually became an elder of the church. Pat routinely attended LDS meetings. When some (church) doctrines didn't seem right to her, Pat would just think back to the audible voice she had heard earlier.

John and Pat felt a strong need to make a pilgrimage to the Mormon Temple in Salt Lake City to renew their wedding vows inside the most sacred building in Mormonism. Church leadership informed them that they had to go through a formal meeting with church officials in order for them to get "a temple recommend." [354] In doing so, Pat and her husband had to acknowledge (and prove) that they gave ten percent of their gross income to the Church. They also had to promise that they did not drink alcohol, coffee or tea.

The Whites were thrilled when they were granted permission to go inside the Salt Lake City Temple. To their delight, they would be getting remarried inside the Temple, one of the holiest places on earth according to Mormon theology.

Patricia entered the SLC building Temple several weeks later and became aware of what her Mormon vows really meant. It was explained to her by church officials that marriage within the confines of her church's doctrine taught that one day she would help populate a planet and be one of many wives to her husband. While Patricia saw herself as a good wife, she believed these teachings from her church just didn't make sense.[355]

It bothered Pat to know that her 'eternal marriage' to John, now consecrated in the Temple, permitted and expected her husband to marry other wives in the next 'other life'. She couldn't believe this Mormon Church doctrine was from God.[356] Pat asked herself many times, "In all of this, where was the God of love she remembered hearing about so many years ago as a child?" Pat struggled to think that a God of love would condone this behavior.

Pat's search for "the God of love" made it increasingly more difficult for her to regularly attend her weekly ward meetings. She remembered going into the ward one day, picking up a Book of Mormon and turning the pages of the book to read about the 'abominable church'. Pat recalled inwardly questioning "I wonder if this is the abominable church?"

Patricia's quest for finding the real "God of love" led her to talk to her younger brother, Tony who sent her a copy of the 1980's book, The God Makers.[357] Pat decided to find her own conclusions. She became convinced that her church contained many inconsistencies. Patricia believed something to be wrong with the way Mormonism portrayed women. She commented, "I had no doubt the Mormon Church was false and not the only true church." The exclusivity of the church doctrine puzzled Pat. She felt an urgency to talk to someone who had already gone through the experience of leaving the Mormon faith.

The Journey Away From Mormonism

Pat eventually talked with Dolly and Chuck Sackette who had come out of the Mormon Church earlier. Since the Sackette's weren't in town at the time, Pat decided to meet with their daughter. Pat shared with the Sackette's daughter her story of a lady who had once wanted her to accept Jesus as her Lord and Savior. Pat admitted that she just couldn't make a decision for Christ at that time. Sackette's daughter told Pat that if she ever wanted to go to heaven, she'd have to accept Christ as her Savior. It wasn't long before she would pray,

"Dear Heavenly Father, I don't understand if this is the only way to go to heaven, I want to receive Jesus Christ as my Savior and Lord." [358]

At first, nothing happened, so she thought a week later she would try again. In her own words she explained, "It wasn't until then that things started to happen." As she looked around her neighborhood, she noticed that "all the colors I saw were much brighter, more defined." Pat shared, "I was full of marvelous, magnificent joy," a unique joy she hadn't ever experienced before for she had encountered Jesus Christ. [359]

During the summer of '85, Pat just wanted to talk about Jesus Christ. "She wanted to tell everyone about Jesus... whether people were in stores, on planes, on the streets or anywhere." She knew in her heart that what she had found was real ... She knew she had experienced a profound encounter with the Christ of the Bible. [360]

Patricia's old friends at the ward reported her to the local Mormon Bishop. Within days, the leader of her former church warned Pat not to tell other church members about her new faith, however Pat felt compelled to talk about her "born again" experience. The church approached her a second time and demanded that she stop sharing her faith with other Mormons. Pat had always obeyed the church in the past but this time was different. She just could not do it! She told the Mormon leader "Nobody is going to stop me from taking about Jesus."

Several weeks passed before a private letter came to the Whites from church leadership requesting a meeting. Patricia felt that after her almost twenty years of service and allegiance to the Church of the Latter Day Saints, she deserved an opportunity to explain her position. The leaders decided to grant her a formal hearing.

During the hearing Mormon leadership asked Pat if she believed that Joseph Smith and Brigham Young were true prophets of God. Pat told them that she believed that neither of these men were true prophets of God, for how could they be? Joseph Smith once said, "God made Aaron to be the mouth-piece for the children of Israel and He will make me a god to you in His stead ... and if you don't like it, you must lump it." [361] Pat asked herself just one question. How could these leaders place their faith in such a fallible man?

201

Patricia soon sent Mormon leadership a three-page letter explaining why she wanted to leave the LDS Church. Pat explained, "I have found it very interesting that having gone to the Temple for nineteen years, and not once when I was interviewed, not once, had anyone ever asked me if I believed in Jesus Christ." Patricia White was excommunicated from the Mormon Church by the end of the summer in 1985.[362]

Her husband and daughter, Beth, soon joined Pat. Pat's oldest daughter Leslie, however met an LDS man in Moorpark whom she would eventually marry. Leslie now has six children and is still part of the LDS church.[363]

It didn't take long for John and Pat to begin meeting with other born-again believers in a small Baptist Church in Moorpark. Patricia's whole outlook on life began to change. She now had a profound peace which sharply contrasted from her days of occasional struggles with depression. The only explanation Pat offered for this dramatic change was that she had now met her Creator. Patricia knew, beyond a doubt, that the same loving God she met that day in Moorpark took over as the greatest part of her life!

As Pat found direction through prayer and reading the Bible, God began speaking through the pages of her Bible. As she began to avidly read the story of Christ, she learned what it meant to truly be a Christian. She understood the Bible to be a spiritual book and best understood by those who are willing to hear God speak to them through its pages.

By 1988, Pat's husband John decided to retire from United Airlines. The couple chose to sell their home in Moorpark and retire to San Diego, California.[364] After their move Pat became a strong advocate of the Pro-Life movement in the city. Pat and John regularly joined their friends on Saturday mornings outside local abortion clinics peacefully showing support for the unborn. Pat believes that it is important to express her right to assemble and speak defending the unborn; and pleaded with mothers not to abort. She would do so even if it meant arrest and jail for her beliefs.

Patricia could never fully understand why so many Christian pastors seemed afraid to publicly decry a medical procedure that has destroyed the lives of more than forty-five million infants since 1973. After years of involvement with groups like Operation Save America, Pat decided to donate her time by teaching English to deprived Mexican children at a Christian orphanage in Tijuana. Her work in the orphanage became a rewarding experience during her later years.[365]

On May 9, 2011, Patricia Louise White went home to be with her Lord and Savior, Jesus Christ. Months before her death John still remembers his wife actively sharing her Christian faith with anyone who cared to listen. Her long time friend, Heather Mechanic, also has fond memories of the many times Pat shared the good news of Jesus Christ that she had first experienced so many years ago back in Moorpark. Even after all her years in the LDS church, Pat's heart continued to reach out to the Mormon people, and present the gospel message of the Bible to counter the false hope the Book of Mormon offers them. Patricia made and kept a commitment to pray for her Mormon friends every day.[366]

Ultimately, she knew that only the true Jesus of the Bible can offer the peace, love and direction that mankind now so desperately needs. The bottom line is that truth is truth, and there can only be one truth when it comes to eternity.

Chapter 16

The Rich Man and Lazarus A Trip to Hell

This final amazing story is about two persons who lived almost 2,000 years ago. One of these persons could be you! While this amazing story is somewhat different than the modern-day sagas we have been exploring, it's real and life-changing. I encourage you as you read this story to make an important decision about your own amazing story.

Luke 16 contributes just one of many parts of the New Testament that illustrates some of the important spiritual insights Jesus of Nazareth told his faithful followers. One famous passage found in the verse 13 reads, "'No one can serve two masters. For you will hate one and love the other; you will be devoted to one and despise the other. You cannot serve both God and money." [367] By this Jesus asserted that each one of us must determine whom we will serve—God, or something else. The Jewish teacher attempted to communicate the importance of how God should have first place in our hearts (instead of money, people, things, or whatever).

Even before Christ tells the story of the rich man, he reminds his followers of just how deeply God loves each one of us. In the fifteenth chapter of Luke, Christ clearly tells three distinct parables. (Webster says a parable is a short fictitious story that illustrates a religious principle or theme). [368] Jesus used these three parables, (the parable of the lost sheep, the parable of the lost coin and the parable of the prodigal son), to show just how far God will go to reach out and touch our lives. Perhaps the use of these parables in the previous chapter explains why some Biblical scholars believe the story of "the rich man" is also a parable. However, in contrast, it is not a parable at all.

Jesus recounted the true story of a rich man by beginning his narrative saying, there was a certain rich man. While we are not given the name of this person, we know from Jesus' words that he once lived on earth and he was a man of personal wealth. The preface word makes it clear that Jesus knew of him, as he was referred to as a certain man. Webster's dictionary defines certain as "particular ... specific" so we know that the Jewish teacher knew about this man's life.

The man in the story dressed himself in fine linen and purple. The Old Testament assigns the color purple to expensive articles and garments usually worn of royalty. It was "a rich material dyed with the liquid obtained from the shelled murex." [369] The purple murex and the fine linen clothing cost a pretty penny in those days. Jesus went on to say that this man fared "sumptuously every day." We know by Jesus' own words that this man livid luxuriously and lavishly during this stage of his life. [370]

We also know by Jesus' true story that during this same period in time, a beggar named Lazarus also lived. Unlike the rich man, Lazarus lived a very meager life. He regularly begged for food at the city gate in the same locale where the rich man would sometimes pass. Lazarus became so hungry that he "longed for scraps from the rich man's table." Jesus tells us that as Lazarus begged at the city gate even some of the "dogs would come and lick his open sores."

The story continues. Jesus then pulled open the veil between the spiritual and physical worlds we live in. Jesus Christ, the one whom John the Baptist refers to as 'the Lamb of God' (John 1:29) tells his followers in Luke 16:22 that both men died. When the poor man (Lazarus) died he was carried by the angels to be with Abraham. (Abraham's walk with God was written about extensively in pages of the Old Testament of the Bible and he lived centuries before the birth of Christ. While considered to be the spiritual father of the Jewish people, his strong faith in God serves as a great model to all of us).

Jesus then explained that "the rich man also died and was buried: and in hell he lifted up his eyes, being in torments...." The eternal destiny of both of these men reminds us of Jesus' warning about the reality of heaven and hell. In the ensuing passages Jesus described this place of the dead, as a place of "torments, suffering and flame(s) ..." and a terrible end for those who reject God's grace and forgiveness during their lifetime on earth.

Christ pictured this place of torment as one of several spiritual destinations spoken about in the Bible. Even using Jesus' own words, many critics still negate hell's existence. In an April 2011 Time Magazine article titled 'What if Hell Doesn't Exist?' the publication put forth the assertion of Hell as a myth. Many critics fail to understand that Christ spoke on this subject on numerous occasions and even granted us a glimpse of this reality with the story of the rich man in Luke.

During his relatively short, three-year ministry, Jesus warned us about this place of destruction. He routinely told his followers about the negative consequences of rejecting God. Sadly, many ministers today are reluctant to warn their congregations of hell's reality. Many priests and religious leaders from around the globe are more interested in political correctness than declaring the truth about eternity. People from all over the world who want to know the truth about what Jesus said need only know that an eternal destination awaits everyone—either heaven or hell.

The Bible teaches that God created hell for Lucifer and his angels. But sadly, it has also become the eternal destination for unbelievers. Eternal separation from God awaits those who have rejected God's greatest gift to mankind – His son, Jesus Christ. Jesus came to earth for the purpose of bridging the separation that exists between God and mankind. God's gift to mankind was His son who died on the Cross for our sins.[371] God continually tries to reach out to each of us with His message of love and salvation but God will not force His love on us. True love offers a voluntary—not forced—choice.

Jesus' disciple Matthew, the former tax collector, quoted this admonition to us in Matthew 7:13-14 (NIV), "Enter through the narrow gate. For wide is the gate and broad is the road that leads to destruction, and many enter through it. But small is the gate and narrow the road that leads to life, and only a few find it." [372] Judgment Day will be bitter for the multitudes who never found the narrow gate, as on that day, it will be too late.

Just like his story about the rich man and Lazarus, Christ unveiled the reality of life after death. He conceded that most reject God's love and take the road that leads to destruction. The rich man who ignored God and loved his wealth more demonstrates this lack of wisdom. The rich man lived for himself and his pleasures. Once he realized his fate, he begged Abraham for mercy, but for him life on earth, as he knew it, was over. God's mercy is extended to each one of us – during our lifetime—but not afterward.

Before Christ recounted the story of the rich man and Lazarus, he reminded us in Luke 15 how much God desires to be in fellowship with us. The story of the prodigal son illustrates this very well. God uses this story to demonstrate His wells of compassion and deep unconditional love.

Are You on the Path to an Undesired Destination?

By the time the rich man died, it didn't take long for him to realize where he was and that life, as he knew it on earth, was over. He knew something felt very wrong for now he stood in a place of torments ... and fire. Clearly by Jesus' reenactment of the story the people "can remember...They are thirsty. They can see and hear. They can think and feel pain" in hell. [373]

The rich man realized he didn't want to be to be there nor did he want his brothers to come to such a place. Like the rich man, many of us still don't heed Christ's warnings found in Matthew 7:13. The rich man had the opportunity of turning to God during his lifetime but, instead, rejected the words of the prophets and the words of Moses that encouraged him to make God a priority in his life. This is why Christ asks us to seriously consider, "What good will it be for someone to gain the whole world, yet forfeit their soul?" [374] Or what can anyone give in exchange for their soul? The rich man placed his riches over a relationship with God. It should be emphasized that you don't have to be rich to place money above God. It should also be noted that while the love of money can become an idol, there are many other idols that people place before God as well. The Bible tells us, "For the love of money is a root of all kinds of evil. Some people, eager for money, have wandered from the faith and pierced themselves with many griefs." [375]

This is not to say that money is evil, as of course it can be used for many wonderful purposes. Obviously we need to earn money to live and provide for our families. Scripture does tell us, though, that "the love of" or lust for money can have damaging spiritual and eternal consequences.

The Bible also calls it wrong to place anything in front of our relationship with God. For some, like the 'rich man' it was money; for others it might be power, relationships, addictions, prestige, pride, or selfishness at the top of our priorities. There are many ways to be distracted from pursuing God. But the important thing to remember is that God is always there. He is always reaching out to us with His love. We must not ignore Him. It serves us well to learn from the mistakes that the rich man made.

During his lifetime on earth, the rich man also didn't have compassion for the troubled needy man, Lazarus. The rich man put himself first. He did not and would not express any compassion for the poor beggar. Luke chapter 16:19-31 shows us that, we cannot "assert that the mere possession of wealth is wrong or that mere poverty justifies. On the contrary, the rich man received condemnation, not because he was rich, but because he was callous, and Lazarus justified, not because he was poor, but because he was poor in spirit. The callousness of the rich man was due to his skepticism. He consumed his wealth in selfish luxury, sparing none of it for the poor, because he did not really believe in God or a future life." [376]

After the rich man died, his soul journeyed into eternity ... But after he died, Jesus tells us that he remembered his brothers, who still lived. This clearly indicates that the man retained his memory in this other dimension. He had entered a spiritual place where he experienced total awareness of himself and those things around him. Knowing his location, the rich man suddenly was concerned about his eternal destiny. He wanted to warn his brothers of his condition but he could not. It was too late.

Abraham reminded the rich man that his brothers, like himself, had the same Biblical writings of Moses and teachings of the prophets that he had. Like the rich man, his brothers showed more concern about worldly things. The rich man's insight told him that trouble lay ahead for his brothers because they didn't care about God's love for them or the words of the prophets and teachings of Moses. How sad! How panic stricken he must have felt to realize that his loved ones were also doomed!

Jesus' sermon reminds us that our time on earth is ultimately important but also finite and limited. Jesus tells us two great Biblical truths from the New Testament. "Love the Lord your God with all your heart and with all your soul and with all your mind and with all your strength.' The second is this: 'Love your neighbor as yourself.' There is no commandment greater than these." [377] Clearly these verses tell us that our relationship with our Creator is the most important relationship we can have.

The true story of the rich man tells us that eternity is real. When we physically die, we will journey into the spiritual realm. At the end of our last breath, we will be in the presence of God. It is at this moment that eternity is revealed and we will either be forever with God or forever separated from Him. Jesus makes it clear that we have to make a choice but that choice must be made while we are alive. The Bible teaches us, "For the wages of sin is death, but the gift of God is eternal life in Christ Jesus our Lord." [378] "Jesus Christ is the only provision for man's sin. Through Him, you can know and experience God's love and plan for your life." [379] Jesus revealed, "I am the way and the truth and the life. No one comes to the Father except through me." [380]

Of all the world's major religions, Christ is the only main religious figure who has conquered death. After his resurrection, (three days after his death on the cross), Christ appeared publicly to over 500 people. Hearing that the Nazarene had been raised from the grave, Thomas, the doubter, said, "Unless I see the nail marks in his hands and put my finger where the nails were, and put my hand into his side, I will not believe." [381] This account goes on to say that when Thomas saw the risen Christ for the first time a week later, He instructed Thomas to "put your fingers here … look at my hands, then stretch out your hand and put it on my side." Thomas saw Christ's death. He knew of his burial but felt totally overwhelmed by the miracle that he saw before him. He reacted the only way that he could by addressing Jesus, "My Lord and my God." Thomas later went on to become the only disciple of the twelve to spread the gospel outside of the Roman Empire.

Most all of Christ's twelve Disciples who followed him during his three years of public ministry, ended up dying violent deaths as martyrs because of their belief in Jesus Christ the Messiah. You need to seriously ask yourself, 'If the claims of Christ's resurrection were false, why would these men who walked with him for three years allow themselves to be executed just to defend a lie?'

You Can Confess the Truth!

In closing, Jesus' story of the rich man and Lazarus clearly demonstrates that "the life of all men … is continued without interruption after the separation of soul and body" upon death. [382] We choose our eternal destiny. God places this decision before each of us in many different ways every day. But ultimately, it is a choice each one of us must make before we die. It should be abundantly clear that as human beings we are in desperate need of a Savior. He is available whenever you are. When He becomes your personal Lord and Savior, your own story will become amazing for all eternity!

A Final Word The Most Amazing Story Can Be You

B ack in the 1950s Bill Bright, founder of Campus Crusade for Christ, put together a small fifteen page booklet entitled, "The Four Spiritual Laws." Bright wrote the booklet to simply summarize the Christian message of salvation. He included in the small book's text a number of key Bible verses that support the need for personal salvation in Christ.

The message that Dr. Bright put together in this booklet; of which two billion copies[383]have been distributed throughout the world, was instrumental of changing my life as well. It is a simple message that (1) God loves you and offers a wonderful plan for your life, (2) Man is sinful and is separated from God. (3) Jesus Christ is God's only provision for man's sin. Through him you can know and experience God's love and plan for your life, and finally (4) we must individually receive Jesus Christ as Savior and Lord (then we can know and experience God's love and plan for our lives).[384]

Throughout the New Testament of the Bible, the apostle Paul recounted his dramatic conversion to Christ: from a persecutor of Christians to one of the first centurie's most famous evangelists and followers of Christ. Paul (Saul of Tarsus) had a remarkable story. He discovered the meaning of life.

Even though the times have changed, that same message of love and is still extended to mankind everywhere. Today the Creator of the Universe is actively reaching out to those who seek Him. Just like the story of Paul, He uses the stories of real men and women to reveal Himself to each of us today; if we choose to hear from Him. Just as the stories from the book demonstrated how God reached out to these individuals, God also wishes to reach out to you.

The same God who touched the lives of all of the people that are featured in this book is available to all of us. He is actively seeking a relationship with each of His precious creations. Almost 2 thousand years ago, He went so far as to come down to mankind's level by revealing himself in human form (Jesus Christ) and dying for each one of us on the Cross. His death is spoken of in the Bible in 1 Corinthians 15:3-6:

"Christ died for our sins, just as the Scriptures said. He was buried, and he was raised from the dead on the third day ... He was seen by Peter and then by the twelve. After that he was seen by more than 500 of his followers." Christ Himself said, "I am the way, the truth, and the life; no one comes to the Father but through Me. (John 14:6). [385]

As the real people in this book discovered, it is not enough to know these simple Bible truths. It is important for each one of us to act on them and actively follow the Christ of the Bible and allow Him to be in control of our lives. I encourage each one of you, in your own personal search for meaning, purpose and truth to act on this. It will be a decision that will forever change your life for the better!

About the Author

James ('Lee') Lambert grew up in San Diego (California), graduating from high school at La Jolla Country Day School. The author attended Linfield College in McMinnville, Oregon and received a Bachelor of Arts degree. Additionally, he has received his Masters in Business Administration from National University (San Diego). Lambert previously worked in various management capacities for Crocker National Bank, San Diego Trust & Savings Bank and First Interstate Bank. He also taught Finance at Mira Costa Community College for three years. James also served as a bank credit analyst for a year where he developed a knack for writing. In 1997, he released his first book Porn in America, published by Huntington House Publishers. He has appeared on the O'Reilly Factor twice, Hardcopy (Paramount Pictures), The Morning Show (BBC-TV), The Crier Report (Court TV), the 700 Club twice (ABC family channel), The Morning News (Fox News Channel), the Trinity Broadcasting Network (six times), CBN News Brief (ABC family channel) and 100 Huntley Street (CTS television – Canada) twice. He has also appeared on numerous local radio and television stations over the years and presently.

Lambert writes commentary for www.RenewAmerica.com, www.OneNewsNow.com, and www.ChristianMirror.net . He is also the host for a local weekly (Sunday night), cable television show called "Night Lights" in San Diego. Lambert is a licensed RE loan sales agent and has a strong background in real estate lending, retail and commercial lending. He is married and has two children.

The author can be contacted by going to his website www. JamesLLambert.com or by calling him at his toll free number 1-800-656-8603 or by writing to P.O. Box 12, La Jolla, CA. 92038. He is available for interviews regarding his newest book, 16 Amazing Stories of Divine Intervention (www.16AmazingStories.com) and the encouraging stories contained within its pages.

Endnotes

C ontact can be made with many of the personalities that are featured in the book who are still with us. I encourage you to reach out to those who are available and others who are still in the ministry. Further, you are welcome to further delve into the stories of each of these individuals considering your interest in their stories.

In the reference section of this book there are many excellent citations, book references and web sites that will allow you to inquire further into the stories of these remarkable people. For music lovers, I encourage you to either contact or go to the websites of musicians who are featured in the book (Brian Welch, Bryan Maclean and Oden Fong.) All three offer wonderful discs of their music that is available to the public.

[1] Sport Illustrated Magazine, p. 72, April 18, 1994.

[2] Mickey Mantle, All My Octobers, (New York: Harper, 1994) p. 8.

[3] Mickey Mantle: http://en.wikipedia.org/wiki/Mickey_Mantle 09/08/2009

[4] Lambert, James. "Mickey Mantle's 11th Hour Miracle" Agapepress.org 08/12/2005

[5] Merlyn, David, Mickey Jr., Dan Mantle, A Hero All His Life, (New York: HarperCollins, 1994) p. 39.

[6] Posnanski, Joe. Sport Illustrated www.sportsillustrated.cnn.com "Talkin' Matt Wieters and the concept of Hype" June 1, 2009.

[7] Merlyn, David, Mickey Jr., Dan Mantle, A Hero All His Life, p. 40.

[8] Ibid, p. 41.

[9] Hevesi, Dennis. "Merlyn Mantle, who was married to Yankee great for 43, Dies at 77" August 12, 2009

[10] Sports Illustrated Magazine, April 18, 1994, p. 72

[11] Mantle, Mickey. All My Octobers

[12] Mantle, Mickey. All My Octobers, p. 29.

[13] Almanac1: www.baseball-almanac.com/ws/yr1955ws.shtml (series summary)

[14] Ibid pp. 47-60.

[15] Almanac2: www.baseball-almanac.com/ws/yr1956ws.shtml (series summary)

[16] Almanac3: www.baseball-almanac.com/ws/yr1958ws.shtml (series summary)

[17] Mantle, Merlyn, Mickey Jr., David and Daniel. A Hero All His Life, p. 16.

[18] Mantle, Mickey. All My Octobers p.105.

[19] Linderman, Bill & Allen, Maury. Our Mickey – Cherished Memories of an American Icon, Triumph Books, Chicago, Ill. 2004 quote by Yogi Berra.

[20] Almanac: www.baseball-almanac.com/ws/yr1961ws.shtml (series summary)

[21] Almanac: www.baseball-almanac.com/ws/yr1963ws.shtml (series summary)

[22] Almanac www.baseball-almanac.com/ws/yr1964ws.shtml (series summary)

[23] Lambert, James. Mickey Mantle's 11th hour miracle www.agapepress.org August 12, 2005.

[24] Schwarz, Alan. "The Day the Tigers Tipped Pitches for the Mick" New York Times 05/09/2009

[25] Mantle, Merlyn, Mickey Jr., David & Dan. A Hero All His Life, p. 19.

[26] Lambert, James. Mickey's Mantle of Faith www.worldnetdaily.com www.worldnetdaily.com/index.php?fa=PAGE.view&pageID=38430 10/19/2006

[27] Ibid.

[28] Sports Illustrated Magazine, April 18, 1994. pp. 81, 66.

[29] Mantle, Merlyn, Micky Jr., David & Dan–Hero All His Life, p. 93.

[30] Lambert, James. "Mickey's Mantle of Faith" www.worldnetdaily.com

[31] Ibid.

[32] Ibid.

[33] Ibid.

[34] Ibid.

[35] Ibid.

[36] Barton, David. The Question of Free Masonry and the Founding Fathers Aledo, TX: Wall Builders, 2005, p. 59.

[37] Ibid., p. 42.

[38] Barton, David. The Bulletproof George Washington Wall Builders, P.O. Box 397, Aledo, Texas, p. 25.

[39] Ibid., p. 56.

[40] Ibid., p. 54.

[41] Cook, Fred. "The Golden book of the American Revolution" New York: Golden Press Publishers & Western Printing and Lithographing Company, 1959, pp. 12-15.

[42] Lindsay, Dennis. "A Call to Prayer"- Christ for the Nations Magazine, October 2011, p. 4.

[43] Rivoire, Mario. "The Life and Times of Washington" Life Magazine Philadelphia: The Curtis Publishing Company, 1967. p. 42.

[44] "George Washington" Britannica: The New Encyclopedia Britannica Vol.28 (15th Edition) Chicago, IL. Encyclopedia Britannica Inc., 2007 "George Washington" Britannica: The New Encyclopedia Britannica Vol.28 (15th Edition) Chicago, IL. Encyclopedia Britannica Inc., 2007.

[45] "George Washington" Britannica: The New Encyclopedia Britannica Vol. 28 (15th Edition) Chicago, IL: Encyclopedia Britannica Inc., 2007. p. 703

[46] Ritchie, Donald A. and Broussard, Albert S. American History, The Early Years to 1877 NY: McGraw-Hill, 2001. p. 228.

[47] George Washington's (Valley Forge) letters by permission from the James Copley Library in La Jolla, CA. 92037, 2009.

[48] Beliles, Mark A. and Stephen K. McDowell. America's Providential History Charlottesville, VA: Providence Foundation, 1989. pp. 164-165.

[49] Ibid. p. 175.

[50] Washington, George. "Thanksgiving Proclamation" (10/13/1789) Congressional News Service.

[51] Johnson, Paul. George Washington . Harper Collins Publishers, 10 E. 53rd, New York, NY © 2005, p. 83.

[52] PBS.org/GeorgeWashington/classroom/slavery3,html

[53] Barton, David. Spiritual Heritage, Tour of the U.S. Capitol, p. 73.

[54] Ibid., p. 74.

[55] The Question of Free Masonry and the Founding Fathers, p. 111.

[56] Ibid., p. 112.

[57] Washington's Presidential Farewell Address 09/16/1796 www.csamerican.com/doc.asp?doc=washfarewell#pt1

[58] www.goodreads.com/quotes/show/97756

[59] Morse DD, Jedidiah. Prayer and Sermon on the Death of George Washington, Published by John Stockdale Piccadilly, 1800.

[60] Spiritual Heritage, Tour of the U.S. Capitol, p. 76.

[61] Terrill, Marshall, Steve McQueen, Portrait of an American Hero (Plexus Publishing Limited, 25 Mallison Road, London, SW11 1BW, printed in Great Britain by Bell & Bain Ltd, Glasgow 993, 2003 & 2008) p. 4.

[62] Ibid. pages 8-9.

[63] Boys Republic: Our Philosophy www.boysrepublic.org/philosophy.html

[64] Terrill, Marshall, Bell and Bain. Steve McQueen, Portrait of an American Rebel[Plexus Publishing Limited, 25 Mallison Road, London SW11 1BW © 1993, 2003 & 2008] page 8.

[65] Steve McQueen www.wikipedia.org/wiki/Steve_McQueen 04/06/09

[66] Terrill, Marshall, Bell and Bain. Steve McQueen, Portrait of an American Rebel [Plexus Publishing Limited, 25 Mallison Road, London SW11 1BW 1993, 2003 & 2008. p. 32.

[67] Neile Adams www.wikipedia.org/Neile_Adams 04/02/09

[68] Wikipedia: www.wikipedia.org/wiki/index.html?curid=2842542

[69] TCM: www.tcm.com/tcmdb/title/15857/The-Magnificent-Seven/

[70] Wikipedia: www.wikipedia.org/wiki/Steve_McQueen

[71] Terrill, Marshall Steve McQueen, Portrait of an American Rebel, p. 184.

[72] Neil Adams www.wikipedia.org/Neile_Adams 04/02/09

[73] Virtual Audio Commentary of The Getaway – Warner Bros. Entertainment 2009

[74] Towering Inferno www.tcm.com/tcmdb/416013/The_Towering_Inferno/

[75] Terrill, Marshall. Steve McQueen: Portrait of an American Rebel. p.285.

[76] Ragsdale Jr., Grady. Steve McQueen, the Final Chapter Ventura, CA: Vision House Inc., 1983. p. 1.

[77] McQueen, Barbara with Terrill, Marshall. Steve McQueen, the Last Mile, Dalton Press Fine Books, Dearfield, Ill. ISBN # 1-85443-227-3 2006, p. 31

[78] McQueen, Barbara w/ Terrill, Marshall. Steve McQueen, the Last Mile, Dearfield, Ill. p. 300.

[79] Minty, Barbara with Terrill, Marshall. Steve McQueen, The Last Mile, Dearfield, Ill., p. 199.

[80] Ragsdale Jr., Grady. Steve McQueen, the Final Chapter Ventura, CA: Vision House Inc., 1983. p. 45.

[81] www.wikipedia.org/wiki/Le_Mans_(film) 04/09/22

[82] Nashawaty, Chris. "Steve McQueen's Last Flight." Entertainment Weekly www. EW.com (Nov. 4, 1994)

[83] Ragsdale Jr., Grady. Steve McQueen, the Final Chapter Ventura, CA: Vision House Inc., 1983. p. 171-172.

[84] Ibid., p. 174

[85] Johnson, Brett. "Steve McQueen turned to quiet life in Santa Paula before 1980 death" Ventura County Star 01/13/08

[86] Ruben De La Torre audio taped interview with author (part 1) December, 2009.

[87] Ibid.

[88] Ibid.

[89] Ibid.

[90] Ibid.

[91] Ibid.

[92] Ibid.

[93] Ibid.

[94] Ibid.

[95] Ibid.

[96] 1 Corinthians 13:4-8 (GNB)

[97] Victory Outreach International "Mission Statement" provided by Lisa Mungaray, VOI minister Relations (on behalf of Phillip La Crue) 04/28/2011.

[98] Ronald Reagan Presidential Library, 40 Presidential Dr., Simi Valley, CA. March 2010

[99] Ronald Reagan Presidential Foundation. Ronald Reagan, an American Hero. New York: Kindersly Publishing, 2001. pp. 28-29.

[100] Kengor, Paul. God and Ronald Reagan, A Spiritual Life New York: Harper Collins Publisher, 2004. pp. 18-19.

[101] Ibid. p. 36.

[102] Ronald Reagan Presidential Foundation. Ronald Reagan, an American Hero, p. 40.

[103] "Follow the Reagan Trail" by PJ Francis www.JournalStandard.com

[104] Ronald Reagan Biography (On the air ...) www.notablebiographies.com

[105] Ibid.

[106] Ronald Reagan Presidential Library, 40 Presidential Dr., Simi Valley, CA.

[107] www.wikipedia.org/wiki/Knute_Rockne_All_American Review of the film: Knute Rockne, All-American

[108] Kengor, Paul. God and Ronald Reagan, A Spiritual Life New York: Harper Collins Publisher, 2004. p.44

[109] Ronald Reagan, an American Hero, p. 36.

[110] Robinson, Peter. How Ronald Reagan Changed My Life New York: Harper Collins Publishers, 2003. p. 26.

[111] www.notablebiographies.com/Pu-Ro/Reagan-Ronald.html

[112] Ronald Reagan Presidential Library, 40 Presidential Dr., Simi Valley, CA. March 2010.

[113] Ibid.

[114] The Campaign www.ronaldreagan.com/campaign.html 04/06/10

[115] www.notablebiographies.com/Pu-Ro/Reagan-Ronald.html

[116] The First Term www.ronaldreagan.com/firstterm.html 04/14/10

[117] The Second Term www.ronaldreagan.com/secondterm.html 04/15/10

[118] Ibid.

[119] K. Skinner, A. Anderson & M. Anderson. In His Own Hand- New York: The Free Press, New York, NY, 2001. pp. 359-360.

[120] The Ronald Reagan Foundation. Ronald Reagan, an American Hero San Diego: Tehabi Books, San Diego, CA 2001. p. 140-141.

[121] Ibid. p. 144.

[122] Ronald Reagan Presidential Library, 40 Presidential Dr., Simi Valley, CA. March 2010

[123] Kengor, Paul. God and Ronald Reagan, A Spiritual Life, p.152.

[124] Ed Meese (former US Atty. General under Reagan) audio telephone interview w/ author 03/10/2010.

[125] Robinson, Peter. How Ronald Reagan Changed My Life New York: Harper Collins Publisher, 2003, p. 38.

[126] Kengor, Paul. God and Ronald Reagan, A Spiritual Life New York: Harper Collins Publisher, 2004. p. 184.

[127] Ed Meese (former US Atty. General under Reagan) audio telephone interview w/ author 03/10/10.

[128] Ibid.

[129] SDI www.RonaldReagan.com/sdi.html p. 2.

[130] Ronald Reagan Presidential Library, 40 Presidential Dr., Simi Valley, CA – information gleaned from various displays in the library, March, 2010.

[131] Ibid.

[132] Michael Reagan audio (telephone) interview with author 03-10-2010.

[133] Hymn: Jerusalem – credits: Charles Parry and William Blake, 1916

[134] Oden Fong taped interview with author (part 1) May 2009

[135] www.Imdb.com Benson Fong: biography and movie/TV appearance list

[136] Oden Fong taped interview with author (part 1) May 2009.

[137] Ibid.

[138] Ibid.

[139] Lisa McDaniel (Oden's sister) written communication with author May 30, 2009

[140] Interview with Oden Fong, November 1998 www.one-way.org/jesusmusic/interviews/fong/fonginterview.htm

[141] Oden Fong audio taped interview with author (part 1) May 2009

[142] Japenga, Ann. "Rear View: Turn on, Turn in, Drop out" by Ann Japenga, Palm Springs Life, www.PalmSpringsLife.com November 1988.

[143] Faulds, Mary. "The Beat Goes On" The American Family Association Journal. Tupelo, Miss. April, 2010, p. 18.

[144] Oden Fong audio taped interview with author (part 2) May, 2009.

[145] Ibid.

[146] Taoism: www.answers.com (Taoism) June, 2010

[147] Ibid.

[148] One-Way.org interview (Fong), November, 1998. pp. 1-11.

[149] Oden Fong audio taped interview with author (part 2) May 2009

[150] One-Way.org interview (Fong), November, 1998. pp. 1-11.

[151] Oden Fong audio taped interview with author (part 1) May 2009

[152] One-Way.org interview (Fong), November, 1998. pp. 1-11.

[153] Typed written notes from Oden Fong to the author 09/27/11

[154] Oden Fong interview with the author (part 2) May 2009.

[155] Oden Fong written notes to author (part 3) April 2011

[156] Oden Fong interview with the author (part 2) May 2009

[157] Ibid.

[158] "The Jesus Movement" Time Magazine 06/21/1971, p. 56.

[159] Oden Fong audio taped interview with author (part 2) May 2009

[160] "The Jesus Movement" Time Magazine 06/21/1971, p. 61.

[161] Oden Fong audio taped interview with author (part 2) May 2009

[162] Oden Fong audio taped interview with author (part 3) May 2009.

[163] Mar, Alex. "KoRn's Head Sees Light" Rolling Stone online – pp. 1-2. www.rollingstone.com/news/story/7622829/korn_sees_light

[164] Dickerson, John. "Former KoRn guitarist Brian Welch finds Jesus" Phoenix New Times 06-19-2008

[165] CNN television transcripts – Paula Zahn Now (TV) 12/22/2005

[166] Anderson, Troy. "Head Joins the Body" by Christianity Today 08/13/2007.

[167] MTV news: (Welch) Biography www.MTV.com/music/artist/korn/artist.jhtml

[168] Anderson, Troy. "Head Joins the Body" by Christianity Today 08/13/2007

169 Billboard www.Billboard.com (Biography- Brian Welch)

170 MTV news: (Welch) Biography www.MTV.com/music/artist/korn/artist.jhtml

171 Dickerson, John. "Former KoRn Guitarist Brian Welch Finds Jesus" Phoenix New Times, 06/19/2008.

172 Billboard: www.Billboard.com (biography- Brian Welch)

173 Lambert, James. Personal witness by attendance from author 08/24/1970

174 Bio.com: www.biography.com/articles/Jimi-Hendrix-9334756?part=1

175 CNN television transcripts – Paula Zahn Now (TV) 12/22/2005

176 Dickerson, John "Former KoRn Guitarist Brian Welch Finds Jesus" Phoenix New Times, 06/19/2008.

177 Anderson, Troy. "Head Joins the Body" by Christianity Today 08/13/2007

178 Mar, Alex. "KoRn's Head Sees Light" Rolling Stone online – pp. 1-2.

179 Sing365: Lyrics of A.D.I.D.A.S. by KoRn www.365.com

180 Anderson, Troy. "Head Joins the Body" by Christianity Today 08/13/2007

181 Matthew 11:28 (NIV)

182 Matthew 11:29-30 (NIV)

183 Anderson, Troy. "Head Joins the Body" by Christianity Today 08/13/2007

184 CNN television transcripts – Paula Zahn Now (TV) 12/22/2005

185 Ibid.

186 MTV news: (Welch) Biography www.MTV.com/music/artist/korn/artist.jhtml

187 Ibid.

188 Ibid.

189 Murray, William J. My Life Without God Eugene, OR. Harvest House Publisher, 1992 p.10-11.

190 Murray, William J. My Life Without God Eugene, p. 51.

191 Ibid., p. 55.

192 Rabbi Aryeh Spero, Human Events Magazine 07/20/07

193 Handwritten notes by William J. Murray provided to author 06-10-2011

194 Ibid.

195 Life Magazine (June 9, 1964).

196 Murray, William J. My Life Without God, Eugene, OR: Harvest House Publishers, 1992. p. 120-138.

197 William Murray written notes to author.

198 Murray, William J. My Life Without God, p. 232.

199 Ibid. pp. 300-301.

200 www.ReligiousFreedomCoalition.com

201 Dracos, Ted. Ungodly: the Passions, Torments & Murder of Atheist Madalyn Murray O'Hair

202 www.ReligiousFreedomCoalition.com

203 Annie Meadows (audio) taped interview with author (part 1) 07-01-2009

204 Annie Meadows (audio) taped interview with author (part 1) 07-01-2009

205 Ibid.

206 Ibid.

[207] Handwritten notes from A. Meadows May, 2011

[208] "Witchcraft" – World Book Encyclopedia Chicago, IL: World Book, Inc. 2008, p. 371.

[209] Annie Meadows (typed) written notes from A.M. May, 2011

[210] Ibid.

[211] Annie Meadows (audio) taped interview with author (part 1) 07/01/09.

[212] Ibid.

[213] Annie Meadows typed notes from May 2011.

[214] Ibid.

[215] Annie Meadows (audio) taped interview with author (part 2) 07/01/09.

[216] Annie Meadows (typed) written notes from A.M. May, 2011.

[217] Annie Meadows (audio) taped interview with author (part 2) 07/01/09.

[218] Annie Meadows (typed) written notes from A.M. May, 2011.

[219] Annie Meadows (audio) taped interview with author (part 2) 07/01/2009

[220] Jason Hamilton interview with author February 2011

[221] Tim Stephens interview with author February 2011

[222] www.iamsecond.com/seconds/josh-hamilton/

[223] Tim Stephens (the News & Observer, Raleigh, NC) interview with author February 2011

[224] AP, "Rays feel Hamilton has makings of star" www.cnn/si.com pg. 1 06/02/99

[225] Ibid, p. 2.

[226] Tim Stephens (News and Observer, Raleigh, NC) interview with author February 2011.

[227] Ibid.

[228] Pearlman, Jeff. "Prospect with All the Tools" www.sportsillustrated.cnn.com 06/02/99.

[229] Sheinin, Dave. "New Life at the Plate" The Washington Post

[230] Ibid.

[231] Ibid.

[232] Jason Hamilton interview with the author February 2011.

[233] Nightengale, Bob. "Hamilton on the comeback trail" USA Today

[234] Jason Hamilton interview with the author February 2011. ww.usatoday.com/sports/baseball/al/devilrays/2006-06-06-hamilton-cover_x.htm 6/7/06

[235] www.iamsecond.com/seconds/josh-hamilton/

[236] Jason Hamilton interview with the author February 2011.

[237] Michael Chadwick interview with the author February 2011

[238] Ibid.

[239] Roy Silver interview with the author February 2011

[240] Nightengale,Bob. "Hamilton on the comeback trail" USA Todaywww.usatoday.com/sports/baseball/al/devilrays/2006-06-06-hamilton-cover_x.htm 06/07/06

[241] Ibid.

[242] Roy Silver interview with author February 2011.

243 Michael Chadwick interview with author February 2011.

244 Best, D.Clay. "Johnny Narron's top job: maintaining Josh Hamilton's support system" Victoria Advocate 10-26-1

245 Gwynne: "Josh Hamilton finds strength after misstep in recovery from Addiction" Dallas Morning News 10-4-10

246 www.TexasRangers.com Josh Hamilton #32 / stats

247 Ibid.

248 Aron, Jamie. The Boston Herald 10/23/2010.

249 Michael Chadwick interview with author February, 2010.

250 For more information on Josh and Katie Hamilton's ministry go to www.TriplePlayMinistries.com

251 Michael Glatz taped audio interview with author (part 1) August 2010

252 "How a gay rights leader became straight" By Michael Glatze, World Net Daily 7/3/07 www.wnd.com/index.php?f=PAGE.printable&page=Id42385

253 Michael Glatze taped audio interview with author (part 1) August 2010

254 Dartmouth College www.dartmouth.edu/home/about/history.html 05/23/2011

255 Michael Glatze audio taped interview with author (part 1) August 2010

256 Notes to author from Michael Glatze 2011

257 Michael Glatze audio taped interview with author (part 1) August 2010

258 Michael Glatze audio taped interview with author (part 2) August 2010

259 Jennings, Peter. "Unsafe for America's schools" by Peter Jennings, Human Events Magazine 6/29-09

260 Michael Glatze audio taped interview with author (part 2) August 2010

261 Ibid.

262 www.equalityforum.com "About Us"

263 Gay rights leader quits homosexuality by Art Moore – Word Net Daily, www.wnd.com 07-03-2007

264 Michael Glatze audio taped interview with author (part 2) August 2010

265 Ibid.

266 1 Corinthians 10:13 (NIV)

267 D. Carrington audio taped interview (part 1) with author, 2009.

268 Ibid.

269 Ibid.

270 Ibid.

271 www.Wikipedia.org/wiki/DeWitt_Clinton_High_School 2009

272 D. Carrington audio taped interview (part 1) with author. 2009.

273 Ibid.

274 Ibid.

275 Ibid.

276 handwritten noted by Darren Carrington 05/21/11.

277 D. Carrington audio taped interview with author 2009

278 Ibid.

279 D. Carrington audio taped interview (part 2) with author, 2009.

[280] Ibid.

[281] www.mynfldraft.com 5th round, 1989.

[282] Romans 1:16 (NIV)

[283] D. Carrington audio taped interview (part 2) with author, 2009.

[284] Hand-written notes by Darren Carrington 05/21/11.

[285] D. Carrington audio taped interview (part 2) with author, 2009.

[286] Hand-written notes by Darren Carrington 05/21/11

[287] Ibid.

[288] handwritten noted by Darren Carrington, 05/21/11

[289] D. Carrington audio taped interview (part 2) with author, 2009.

[290] NKJV

[291] Ibid.

[292] Ibid.

[293] handwritten noted by Darren Carrington, 05/21/11.

[294] Elizabeth McKee (Bryan Maclean's mother) interview with the author (part 1), October 2008

[295] Ibid.

[296] Ibid.

[297] Love Story- a Smart Productions film / produced by Chris Hall & Mike Kerry – Interview/quote from film footage. 2008.

[298] Elizabeth McKee interview with author (part 1) October, 2008.

[299] www.BryanMaclean.com/blog.htm

[300] Elizabeth McKee interview with the author (part 1) October, 2008.

[301] Ibid.

[302] Love Story, a Start Productions film/produced by Chris Hall & Mike Kerry (Bryan Maclean) interview quote from film footage.(C) 2008.

[303] Liner notes from Electra Records 'Love" release # 8122-73567-2

[304] Elizabeth McKee interview with the author (part 1) October 2008.

[305] Rolling Stone. Arthur Lee, the mastermind behind the psychedelic pop outfit Love succumbs to leukemia by James Sullivan Aug. 4, 2006 (pg. 2)

[306] Ibid.

[307] Elizabeth McKee interview with author (part 1) October 2008.

[308] Da Capo.–Love. Electra Records, New York, NY ELK 4/20/11.

[309] Weiss, Jeff. "The More Things Change" LA Weekly 05-09-2008

[310] Elizabeth McKee interview with author October 2008

[311] www.bryanmaclean.com Bryan Maclean: short biography by David Hoursden

[312] Elizabeth McKee interview with author (part 2) November, 2008.

[313] Ibid.

[314] Ibid.

[315] Ibid.

[316] Ibid.

[317] www.BryanMaclean.com/blog.htm

[318] Former Playboy Bunny Tells of the Road to Life" NFD Magazine February, 1985

[319] Ibid.

[320] Brenda M. MacKillip interview with author (part 1) 04/21/2011

[321] Ibid.

[322] Ibid.

[323] Handwritten notes from Brenda M. MacKillop 04/29/2011

[324] Brenda Notes: corrections by subject after review of her story 04/20/2011

[325] Brenda M. MacKillop interview with author (part 1) in Ky. 04/21/10

[326] DailyMail: "Playboy opens first Playboy Club in 15 years" – Executive Summary

[327] Fisher, Paul A. "Former Bunny Condemns Playboy Lifestyle by Paul A. Fisher, Catholic Twin Circle weekly magazine 06/22/80

[328] Ibid.

[329] Handwritten notes from Brenda M. MacKillop 04/29/2011

[330] Reisman, Judith A, Soft Porn Plays Hardball Huntington House Publisher, 1991. p. 25.

[331] Ibid.

[332] "Former Playboy Bunny Tells of the Road Back to Life" NFD Magazine February, 1985.

[333] Ibid.

[334] Attorney General's Commission of Pornography (testimony by Brenda Miller MacKillop before the commission)

[335] Former Playboy Bunny Tells of the Road to Life" NFD Magazine February, 1985.

[336] Brenda MacKillop audio interview with author (part 1) in KY. 04/21/10

[337] Former Playboy Bunny Tells of the Road to Life" NFD Magazine February, 1985.

[338] Ibid.

[339] Brenda M. MacKillop interview with author (part 2) 04/21/2010 in KY.

[340] Fisher, Paul A. "Former Bunny Condemns Playboy Lifestyle" by Paul A. Fisher, Catholic Twin Circle weekly magazine. 06/22/80.

[341] Ibid.

[342] Brenda MacKillop audio interview with author (part 2) in Ky. 04/22/10

[343] Ibid.

[344] Patricia L. White interview with author (part 1) July 2008 & Notes from Beth Orellana (05/30/2011)

[345] Ibid.

[346] Handwritten notes from Patricia L. White (page 2) March 2004.

[347] Patricia L. White interview with author (part 1) July 2008

[348] Ibid.

[349] Ibid.

[350] New York's Fair- A Final Report, The Improvement Era by Richard Marshall, December, 1965

[351] Handwritten notes from Patricia L. White (page 7) March 2004.

[352] Patricia L. White interview with author (part 1) July 2008

[353] Joseph Smith- a Prophet of God (no named author of story) www.Mormon.org/ Joseph-Smith/ 04/13/11

[354] Notes from Beth Orellana 05/20/2011

[355] Patricia L. White interview with author (part 2) July 2008.

[356] Ibid.

[357] Handwritten notes from Patricia L. White (page 8) March 2004.

[358] Handwritten notes from Patricia L. White (page 9) March 2004.

[359] Patricia L. White taped interview with author (part 2) July 2008

[360] Patricia L. White taped interview with author (part 2) July 2008

[361] History of the Mormon Church, Vol. 6, 2011 pp. 319-320.

[362] Patricia L. White taped interview with author (part 2) July 2008

[363] Ibid.

[364] Ibid.

[365] Ibid.

[366] Handwritten notes from Patricia L. White (page 7 & page 10) written March 2004

[367] New Living Translation Bible. Tyndale House Publishers, Inc., Carol Stream, Illinois. 2007

[368] Webster's 7th New Collegiate Dictionary, G. & C. Merriam Cp. Publishers, Springfield, Mass. 1967.

[369] One Volume Bible Commentary (33rd Printing) New York: The McMillan Company, 1970. p. 760.

[370] One Volume Bible Commentary, New York, NY The MacMillan Company,1970. p. 760.

[371] From "The Four Spiritual Laws" written by Bill Bright, Campus Crusade for Christ, 375 Highway 74 South, Ste. A; Peachtree City, GA.

[372] Matthew 7:13 NIV

[373] Chick, Jack T. Scream–Chick Publications, Ontario, CA. (year not indicated) p. 10.

[374] Matthew 6:26 (NIV)

[375] 1 Timothy 6:10 (NIV)

[376] One Volume Bible Commentary, the MacMillan Company, 866 3rd Ave, New York, NY (1970) p. 760.

[377] Mark 12:30-31 (NIV)

[378] Romans 6:23 (NIV)

[379] From "The Four Spiritual Laws" written by Bill Bright, Campus Crusade for Christ, 375 Highway 74 South, Ste. A; Peachtree City, GA.

[380] John 14:6 (NIV)

[38] John 20:25 (NIV)

[382] One Volume Bible Commentary (33rd Printing) New York: The McMillan Company, 1970. p. 761-762

[383] www.billbright.com (The Four Spiritual Laws)

[384] Ibid.

[385] Holy Bible–New Living Translation (second edition) Tyndale House Publishers, Carol Stream, Illinois 2007.

CPSIA information can be obtained
at www.ICGtesting.com
Printed in the USA
LVOW13s0002191017
552969LV00024B/702/P